Black Dog, White Couch,
and the Rest of My Really Bad Ideas

Dawn Weber

Beetle Hill Books

BLACK DOG, WHITE COUCH,

AND THE REST OF MY REALLY BAD IDEAS

Copyright © 2020 by Dawn Weber

All rights reserved, including the right to reproduce this book or portions thereof in any form whatsoever. For information, address: Beetle Hill Books, PO Box 65, Brownsville, OH 43721.

Author's note: The events described in this book are mostly true, at least to the best of the author's age-addled memory. Some timelines have been compressed, and some stories exaggerated and satirized for comedic effect. To protect anonymity, some characters have been combined, and some names and identifying characteristics have been changed.

Cover design by Vanessa Maynard

ISBN: 978-0-578-78296-6

Praise for *Black Dog, White Couch, and the Rest of My Really Bad Ideas*

"As a mom of two kids and a dog, I can completely relate to the domestic chaos that ensues in Dawn Weber's hilarious new book, 'Black Dog, White Couch.' It is, in fact, so strikingly familiar and outrageously funny, that it convinced me to get rid of my sofas… and my kids, and just keep the dog. Witty, wry, and with a flair for finding the funny in everyday life, Dawn takes you on an uproarious journey through the craziness that is her family and leaves you laughing and wanting to avoid slipcovers at all costs."
— Tracy Beckerman, syndicated columnist and author of *Lost in Suburbia: A Momoir*

"Dawn's stories reveal the woman we wish was our neighbor. Smart without being stuffy, familiar yet new, the kind of woman you know owns margarita glasses and isn't afraid to use them. 'Black Dog, White Couch' is a fast-reading, short-story trip through one family in America, an unvarnished look into the life of a clever woman and the family and dogs that torture her so."
— Pearl Zambory, author of the chapbooks *I Was Raised to be A Lert* and *The Second Book of Pearl: The Cats*

"Dawn Weber has done it again. I was on my way to purchase new, white furniture. I read her latest book, and owning a black Cocker Spaniel, all thoughts of white furniture were banished. Thanks for saving me, Dawn. That's just the beginning of hilarious, I mean good, advice for those of us with dogs, and/or family, and/or Little Debbie cakes, and/or food, and the wrong furniture. Throw in a couple of parents too. Dawn captures the nitty gritty details of life that most of us choose to ignore. She stops just short of giving advice on hoarding, and I suspect that will be in the next book. If you are alive to the point of breathing, this book will do more than tickle your funny bone. Enjoy it with the following warning: Not to be read while drinking, eating, or being a woman over the age of 60 without your Depends. Thank you, Dawn. We, the world, have been in desperate need of something to laugh at. It might as well be you."
—Wanda M. Argersinger, author of *Southern Mae O'Naze*

"With refreshing candor and a wit that don't quit, Dawn Weber draws us right in to her everyday chaos. Hilarious and relatable, snuggle up in your favorite PJs and grab a fun beverage, because you will not be able to put 'Black Dog, White Couch' down!"
—Janet Frongillo, author of *Mommy Mixology, A Cocktail for Every Calamity*

CONTENTS

1	Black Dog, White Couch	1
2	Missy the Mastiff	6
3	Dethroned	10
4	Whale Tale	13
5	Here–Take My Money	16
6	I Can't See Clearly Now	19
7	Open Mouth, Insert Foot	23
8	I Have Issues	26
9	Hello Kitty	33
10	Dogs With Jobs	39
11	Breaking Bad: The Meth Lab Speaks	42
12	Missy the Mastiff Finds Jesus	45
13	Missy the Mastiff Speaks	49
14	Bacon Envy	52
15	But Who's Counting?	56
16	Life's Too Short to Live in Ohio	59
17	Who Are You People?	62
18	Go Ahead–Throw the Book at Me	66
19	Excuses, Excuses	69
20	I'll Take the Shirt off Your Back	74
21	He Drives Me Crazy	79

22	He Knows Not What He Speaks	82
23	The Country Crock Chronicles	85
24	Spandex: Friend or Foe?	92
25	Pull up a Couch	95
26	TP Apocalypse	98
27	Butt-Washin' Bliss	102
28	Illegal in Several States	106
29	No Clothes? No Problem!	109
30	Hotel Hepatitis	112
31	Jeff Probst: He Haunts Me	116
32	Five Crappy Cars	120
33	Warning: Acronyms Ahead	130
34	The Flaming Fairmont of Death	134
35	Lost Identity: A Tale in Three Parts	138
36	Useful as Well as Ornamental	145
37	My Cell Phone, My Precious	148
38	Domestic Warfare	154
39	I Like to Watch	157

For my Princess.

I saw your signs, and I got back to work.

1
Black Dog, White Couch

I exercise regularly.

I exercise in *futility*, that is.

This I discovered recently, while sweating and grunting in an unladylike fashion near the couch.

"What are you doing?" asked the Husband, lounging in a chair across the room.

I stared at him over the top of a cushion. "What does it look like I'm doing? I'm taking the slipcovers off the couch so I can wash them."

"Wasting your time again, I see," he said. "Didn't you just wash them?"

"Yes, a couple weeks ago. And a couple weeks before that."

He shook his head and glanced at my feet, where our dog, Suzie the Meth Lab, sat drooling, panting and shedding her inky black fur. I could tell he had more to say. But he knew better.

Still, I gave him some direction. "Just be quiet."

The look on his face told me what he was thinking. black dog + white couch = really bad idea.

He had a point. Sometimes I have great ideas–just ask me and I'll tell you. But more often than not, I come up with really bad ideas. Horrible ideas. Terrible ideas. The world's absolute worst ideas.

Since I am so very talented in this area, I decided to write a book about it. Because who am I not to share? I'm a giver, really.

I am so great at bad ideas that sometimes I have them without doing anything at all. Take, for instance, that time I didn't think about my suitcase–until I was halfway to the airport. Or that time I didn't start my senior English term paper–until the day before it was due. Or that time I didn't get the exhaust of my 1982 Ford fixed–until it caught fire.

I know I'm not alone. Everyone has bad ideas; that's just a fact. Everyone feels stupid when plans they've made or actions they've taken—or not taken—turn out to be the wrong ones and as a result, things head straight down the shitter. In life, we're faced with choices every minute of every day, and we can make poor choices, great choices, or neutral choices that don't make a difference at all. Ideas and choices become our actions, and our actions become our successes.

Or colossal failures—my own personal specialty.

My problem is that I'm creative. I don't say this to brag, although being creative is helpful in my day job as a script writer and photographer. I say it because sometimes creativity backfires, especially in the realm of ideas, and especially my ideas. Because creative ideas aren't always the best ideas. Please, take it from me: You should never invest $800 in a 99-cent goldfish. You should never mix mothballs with super glue. You should never simultaneously own a white couch and a black dog. Trust me on this; I speak only the truth. In the upcoming pages, we'll discuss these terrible ideas and more. Many more.

So many more.

Along the way, you'll meet the family: my life-partner, the Husband; our daughter, the sweet-but-spoiled college-age Princess; our son, the Dorito-munching, hygiene-challenged Hobo; and last but not least, our shedding, stinky dogs, Suzie the Meth Lab and Missy the Mastiff.

We'll also cover such years as the 80s—my very own Decade of Dumb—and important topics like my upcoming retirement, impending decrepitude and aversion to pants. These chapters may not be about bad ideas, but they're still important. Hey—everyone gets old, and no one likes pants.

As if all that isn't enough, I'll also give you tips on how you, too, can have bad ideas. You, too, can make poor choices. You, too, can be a moron.

I call such advice my patented "Helpful Guidance™" on what people should and shouldn't do. The Husband calls it "nagging" and "bossing," but he's not "writing" this book. I am, so ignore him. I always do, and it works out great for me.

You'll see that my bad ideas usually start out as what I think are fantastic ideas. As things progress, though, reality sets in, everything turns to crap, and I realize that my fantastic idea was yet another bad idea in disguise. Like that time I rented a hotel room simply because it was cheap. Or that time I bought a totaled car on craigslist from non-English-speaking Russians.

Or that time I bought a white couch. And then another one.

And then several more.

When it comes to the couches, I can't seem to help myself. I've always loved white couches with white slipcovers because they're crisp and clean and look great with any decor.

They're also fussy, time consuming and a huge pain in the ass.

So I bought several of them.

I then apparently looked around at all that crisp, clean whiteness and said, "You know what this place needs? A hyper, ill-mannered dog with inky black fur."

Enter Suzie the Meth Lab, the whirly-twirly bundle of nerves loosely defined as "dog." She's 9 years old now, but still pretty much the same asshole she was as a puppy. She races around! She knocks people over!

She lives life as if it is one big exclamation point!

"I thought she'd have calmed down by now," friends say, studying Suzie's gray chin and pulling claws from their spleens.

In addition to being a spazzy idiot, for quite some time the Meth Lab was under the impression that the clean white sofas weren't our couches. No. They were her beds. Soft, luxurious mattresses on which a dirty black dog could stretch out for a while. There were two in the living room and two in the sunroom. Why, where on earth should she sleep? The choices were many.

After years of yelling, threats and eventually long pine boards placed over the sofas when we left the room, Queen Asshole acquiesced. Now, we, her lowly humans, may use the couches, as long as Her Highness sits plastered against the side of them, near our legs at all times.

Of course, that wasn't the end of our black dog/white couch problems. Trouble continued in the form of loose fur—millions, billions, zillions of strands of dark sticky fur floating around the room in giant tumbling tumbleweeds. Great gobs of hair mating and multiplying and eluding even the best vacuum in its never-ending quest to land . . . where, you ask?

Exactly. All over the white couches.

Purchasing a black dog isn't the only bad idea when you have white couches. Because I now have several and I'm an expert, here is a list of other things not to do:

- Sip red wine
- Eat spaghetti
- Drink chocolate milk
- Trust a questionable fart

And here is a list of things various members of my family have done while on white couches:

- Sip red wine
- Eat spaghetti
- Drink chocolate milk
- Trust questionable farts

These incidents are why I have white slipcovers for the white couches. I say "I" and not "we" because "I" am the one who washes them on a near bi-weekly basis, and washing them really, really "sucks." It is an eight-step procedure that involves sweating, tears, and the occasional zipper-related stab-wound.

Like I said, I'm a white-couch dumbass/expert, so let me give you some Helpful Guidance™ on the slipcover-washing process:

1. Walk into living room toward couch. Bring wine, chocolate milk, spaghetti or another ridiculously dark item, along with ill-mannered dog of questionable hygiene. Ensure that dog has lots of inky black fur.

2. Sit on couch, and accidentally splash wine/chocolate milk/spaghetti all over white fabric. Jump up and curse profusely. This will startle the dog, who, deeply concerned, will leap up and knock you ass-over-tea-kettle back to the couch, where she will excitedly spread fur and spill the rest of your food or beverage.

3. Once blood pressure lowers, rise back up. Retrieve stain remover and begin spraying spots on slipcover. As you spray and wipe, you'll smear the stain and aforementioned dog hair all over the cushion and push it into the fabric. Commence crying.

4. Realize that since you're washing one white slipcover, you might as well wash them all because they all look really bad. Again.

5. Bend over. Pick up cushion and unzip zipper. Now grunt, sweat, pull and curse as you move the fabric, millimeter by stubborn millimeter, off the rubbery, foam-filled seat. Repeat for all six cushions.

Or until you're dead.

6. Throw stained covers in washer with detergent, bleach, OxiClean and more stain remover. Soak for an hour, then start washing cycle. Pray.

Pray hard.

7. Dry slipcovers, and haul all 32 pounds of them back up the stairs. Pick up first cushion, then grunt, sweat, pull and curse to inch cover back over foam until it stops dead halfway through.

8. Tug, jerk and wrench to no avail. Eventually realize you've put the wrong damn cover on the wrong damn cushion. Yank cover off, stab self with zipper and bleed all over the piles of clean white fabric. Grab stain remover and start entire process over. Repeat six to 12 times.

Or until you're dead.

There you have it. It's really not that difficult, right? Why, with just one quick trip to the furniture store, you too can be a complete moron and buy white couches with white slipcovers.

On your way home, grab a bottle of red wine, a gallon of chocolate milk and a big jar of spaghetti sauce. And never, ever, under any circumstances, forget to pick up the most important thing:

A hyper, filthy dog or two.

With inky black fur.

2
Missy the Mastiff

I didn't want another dog.

I even told her, "Mother, I do not want another dog!"

She remained undeterred. "Missy is not your dog. She's my dog."

The problem was that Mother's dogs had a way of becoming my dogs. She knew it, and I knew it. Still, I felt it was worth pointing out again.

"But your dogs always become my dogs!" I shouted into the phone, wasting my breath.

"No," she said. "Not this time. I'm keeping her forever."

I sighed. I didn't want to be mean, but "forever" is a relative term to a 76-year-old woman. Especially one with 24 documented serious health problems, and most especially when said woman had been hospitalized numerous times in recent months.

I did the math. Each hospitalization meant a six-hour whirlwind trip around Ohio from our home in Brownsville to a Youngstown hospital then to Mother's house in New Springfield to pick up her dog du jour and take it. Where? You guessed it:

Back to Beautiful Downtown Brownsville. With me. Where it would become my dog.

This had happened three other times. After the last time, I said, "No more dogs from my mother!"

The Husband said, "No more dogs from your mother!"

Nonetheless, here was my mother fresh from the hospital and on the phone happily telling me, "I got another dog!"

This wasn't just any dog, she said. It was an English mastiff. A big dog. A huge dog. A 154-pound dog.

I repeat, a ONE HUNDRED FIFTY-FOUR POUND DOG.

I slumped over in my chair and cried a little.

"Mom," I said, trying to be gentle, "do you really think that's a good idea? You're so sick most of the time that you have trouble walking across the room. How are you going to walk a dog that big?"

But Mother never let little things like logic stop her. "I'm fine," she scoffed. "Anyway, Missy doesn't need to walk. Mostly, she just lies around."

At that point, I pretty much gave up. The whole conversation was a deja vu, and I knew sooner or later I'd be getting another dog.

A ONE HUNDRED FIFTY-FOUR POUND DOG.

"OK," I said. "You're not going to change your mind. But let me tell you that if you end up in the hospital again and I have to take this dog, you're taking her back. I'm not keeping her. I do not want another dog!"

"Alright!" she yelled. "I'm not going back into the hospital anyway."

Let me ask you, reader. What do you think happened?

Did my mother, with her many and various health problems, go to the hospital again?

Why yes. She did.

Did I drive to Youngstown to see her and then go pick up her enormous dog?

Why yes. I did.

Did my mother get released from the hospital and take her enormous dog back home?

Why no. She didn't.

She up and died on me.

Once again, I found myself with another dog. A giant dog.

A ONE HUNDRED FIFTY-FOUR POUND DOG.

I know, I know—Mother couldn't help it this time. Everyone has to die at some point, and it wasn't her fault she passed away whilst owning a dog as big as a planet.

Well, wait. Yes it was her fault.

Her fault, God's fault—a few weeks after the funeral, whoever's fault it was sat in my living room, drooling while I frantically thumbed through mastiff rescue sites. Few of them seemed to be accepting new dogs. All of them were located in ridiculous places, such as California.

While scrolling, I smelled dog breath and looked up to find Missy the Mastiff staring into my eyes. And I mean directly into my eyes because she was exactly my height as I sat on the couch.

You know, the white couch covered in black hair from the other idiot dog.

"I do not want another dog," I told her.

Missy tilted her head to the left.

"I mean it," I said. "The Meth Lab is enough."

Missy tilted her head to the right.

"Plus, you're way too big!"

Missy licked my face.

And so we have another dog.

Again, this isn't just any dog. She is a dog with her own zip code. A dog with her own ecosystem. A dog with her own weather.

When Missy walked into our house the first day, you could feel her coming from oh, two or three counties away. Her footsteps measured a six on the Richter scale. Structures toppled over. The very earth shuddered beneath her feet.

Suzie the Meth Lab, who usually launches herself onto other dogs at the speed of sound, cowered alone in the corner of the room. You could see the wheels of her tiny brain turn as she wondered: Who is this creature? What is this creature? Will this creature kill me now, or will this creature kill me later?

That was only the beginning for the Meth Lab, the Husband, the kids and me. We all quickly learned many mastiff things from Missy. Many inconvenient, smelly things, such as:

- When the mastiff enters an area, you likely will have to leave because there's not enough space for two. And woe to the person caught between the mastiff and the wall.

  The wall always wins.

- Though they are each the size of a Jeep Cherokee, the mastiff remains unaware of her feet. You, however, will become painfully aware of yours as she smashes, flattens, scratches, crushes, and otherwise destroys them. Cluelessly, she will tramp across your toes on the way outside, whereupon you will collapse on the floor yelling, "Ahhhhhh! You are way too big!"

- When petting, brushing, or even standing in the same hemisphere as the mastiff, it's not unusual to feel moisture on your hands, in your lap and/or directly on your face. As I've said, these dogs produce their own weather, so you might think what you're feeling is rain, perhaps a thunderstorm. You would be wrong.

  You're a victim of Moist Mastiff Drool. Saliva output for these dogs is 100 times that of your average canine and increases exponentially if the victim is wearing a new pair of pants, a fancy dress, or holding an electronic device.

  Thanks to the trails of DNA they leave on the walls, across the floor, down the stairs and in the grass, mastiffs are seldom lost. Moist Mastiff Drool will become one of the reasons you don't have nice things and is best measured with tubs, buckets and/or fire hoses.

- While we're on the subject of fire hoses and reasons you can't have nice things, let us talk about the elephant in the room–and in your yard. I speak, of course, of the Poops. Oh, the Poops. Mastiff Poops.

Yes, Mastiff Poops are so big that they have to be capitalized. No, they're not as bad as you imagine.

They are far, far worse.

Bricks, boulders, masses, mountains—veritable continents of Poops, all around the yard. If you've ever wanted to own a horse with all of the shitty shoveling and none of the awesome riding, these are the dogs for you. True, mastiffs can't help that they emit droppings visible from space. But that's no comfort when you're hoisting turds the size of toddlers.

Despite the above drawbacks, I don't want to give you the idea that sharing a home with a mastiff is all bad. Missy provides tons of comic relief as she fumbles and rumbles around, navigating a universe way too small for her. Particularly amusing is the three-point turn she must execute to leave a space. Observe:

1. Enter area, then discover you don't fit in said area.
2. Attempt to back up. Hit giant ass on wall.
3. Turn head and stare at giant ass in confusion.
4. Move forward. Hit giant head on other wall. Shake giant head in confusion.
5. Repeat several times.
6. Eventually figure out that by angling back and forth, back and forth, you can ever so slightly turn your giant ass/head combo around.
7. Repeat step six over and over, Austin Powers-like, until you can escape.
8. Immediately forget what you just learned, and be on your enormous way.

No, owning a mastiff isn't all bad because the only thing bigger than Missy is Missy's heart. She is unfailingly laid-back, gentle and loyal, and I've always been a sucker for an awesome dog.

Hell, I've always been a sucker for ALL the dogs, and that is why we now have another dog.

A ONE HUNDRED FIFTY-FOUR POUND DOG.

So, for the very last time, Mother's poor decision once again became my poor decision. The Husband, the Hobo, the Princess and I share our space with a colossal, Poops-emitting mastiff/teddy bear, while the Meth Lab, lunatic that she is, runs endless rings around all of us. Because it's too much trouble for her to move, Missy ignores her and spends the bulk of her time chilling out. Mostly, she just lies around. Mother was right.

I hate when that happens.

3
Dethroned

"Hi! How was your day? I missed you."

That's what nice people say when they arrive home from work.

I, however, am not very nice.

"Hey, you! Get off of my couch!"

Startled, the Husband looks up from his phone as I walk in the door. "Hello to you, too. But I believe this is *our* couch, not just yours, madame."

"You know what I'm talking about," I say, hanging up my car keys. "You're in my spot. You're on my chaise."

"Well excuse me, Your Majesty. Let me scoot down."

Crisis averted, I walk over and sit. "Thank you, sir. You are most kind."

"It's not like I had a choice," he grumbles.

I sink in and take a moment to appreciate the comfort, the chaise. This thing is relatively new, but I'd been ogling chaises online for years. It's just another one of my terrible ideas, the latest addition to our arsenal of slipcovered white furniture, which, as you know, are being steadily and cheerfully destroyed by the Meth Lab, her black fur, and the other smelly dog.

To be fair, this is not a true chaise; true chaises are way too expensive. You can buy two couches for the price of one chaise, which is how we ended up with something called an "L-shaped sectional sofa." Because we can't afford the real deal, I have laid claim to the protruding part of the couch and dubbed it my chaise because I am fancy, and I pronounce it "shayze" like the fancy damn person I am. Not "chase" like some kind of illiterate hillbilly.

There are rules.

The problem is not everyone around here seems to know the rules. The problem is they all seem to think they can sit on my chaise. They are wrong, but that doesn't seem to stop them from trying.

The Meth Lab, for one, feels she's entitled to the chaise. I often catch her nestled deep under my creamy-white blanket, sleeping and dreaming and generally being filthy.

Not to be outdone, the Hobo stomps down the stairs each morning, grabs one of his gross Little Debbie snack cakes, and parks himself on my chaise for some Instagramming. This leads to crumbs and a mess, which in turn leads to me yelling while he runs away in a flurry of gross Little Debbie snack cakes.

Then, of course, there's the Husband, who despite my repeated Helpful Guidance™ on where he should and ABSOLUTELY SHOULD NOT sit, parks himself directly on my chaise every single night, whereupon I arrive home and give him additional Helpful Guidance™ in the form of "Get off!" which he, in turn, ignores the next damn night.

Although she happily drools on it, about the only one who doesn't sit on it is Missy the Mastiff. Then again, she doesn't really need it—Missy is a couch unto herself.

The irony of the whole chaise/couch situation is that I am the only person in this household who thought we needed one. The Husband, the Hobo and the Princess believed the other three white couches were enough. They were terribly and woefully wrong, but that didn't keep them from ridiculing me. They scorned, derided and mocked me, all the way up to the day I ignored them and brought it home anyway.

"Why do we need another couch?" asked the Hobo, as he carried his end of the box into the living room.

"It's not a couch," I replied. "It is a *chaise*."

"That's funny because it says right here on the box 'L-shaped Sectional Sofa.'"

"Sofa, couch, whatever. This part," I gestured to the furniture's protruding section on the box's picture, "is going to be mine and it will be my chaise. You and your Little Debbies stay off. No Hobos allowed."

He snorted and put his side of the box on the floor. "Fine, Mother. I will stay off of your chase."

"It is pronounced *shayze* because it is *fancy*," I said. "Get it right."

The Husband stood to the side, hands on his hips. "Another white couch. The dogs are just going to ruin it, too."

"Did I ask for your opinion?" I said. "Anyway, this one is different because you can put your feet up on the chaise. Rather, I can put my feet up on it. Since you two think it's so unnecessary, like I said, stay off."

"Yes, my queen," said the Husband, turning to address the Hobo. "Come, Son. Let us assemble this 'sectional sofa' for Her Highness."

The Hobo bowed and gestured toward the words on the box. "Sure,

Father, but make sure you get the name right," he said. "It is an '*L-Shaped*' sectional sofa."

Then, they giggled. They snickered. They chortled and snorted. *Laugh all you want, minions,* I thought. *Just help me put it together.*

And put it together we did, about six months ago. Tonight I sit, warm and snug, upon my couch, my throne, my "L-shaped Sectional Sofa," my shayze.

I stretch my legs and yawn. "Ahhh. This feels so good."

The Husband looks over at me, concerned. "You know," he says, "sometimes I think you like your chaise more than you like me."

"That's not true," I say. *Then again,* I think, *maybe it is.*

After all, each night when I come home, shoo him away and sit on the chaise, I moan gratefully. I pull on a blanket, remove my bra and pants and fall asleep on top of it, drooling from the side of my mouth. These are all things he'd like me to do with him.

Aside from the drooling, that is.

I laugh and lean deep into the cushions. Puzzled by my merriment, the Husband shakes his head and turns back to his phone, banished to the other end.

Which is, of course, where he damn well belongs.

4
Whale Tale

It had started as a good day. I woke up, did some writing, and even managed to put on pants before noon.

I generally avoid pants, before noon, afternoon, at noon—whenever. But I'd put them on to go kayaking with a friend because pants-free kayaking is not legal in Ohio. You have to travel to, like, California for that crazy shit.

Remind me to check the airfare.

Anyway, it was starting out as a great day, even with the pants. My friend Mechelle and I launched our kayaks at 10 and traveled down the Licking River, marveling at the wildlife and talking about husbands, thrift stores and kitchen gadgets. We are both rabid fans of two of these things.

After a few hours of kayaking and discussing our great loves—thrift stores and kitchen gadgets—we reached our pick-up point, pulled our boats up the bank and loaded them into my truck.

And it was here, right here, when the day went straight to hell.

Because I became a whale.

Let me repeat: I became a whale. A gross, fat whale.

According to my son's friend, that is. I discovered this because as Mechelle and I were climbing into the truck, my son's best friend Adam texted me.

Max Garver says you look like a whale. Just thought you should know. He said he's sorry.

"What the hell?" I said, handing my phone to Mechelle. "The Hobo's friend called me a whale?"

She took the phone, looked at the message and burst out laughing. "Well," she said, "we did just get out of the water . . ."

I started the truck and pulled out of the parking lot, confused.

"Really, though—what the hell? Is Max Garver saying I'm fat? And why is Adam even telling me this?"

"Ha! Better you than me!" she said, wiping away tears.

She was enjoying this. So despite being insulted, I pretended to laugh too. But as I said—what the hell? Why was a 16-year-old boy telling me another 16-year-old boy said I resemble a whale?

Anyway, I knew that Max liked me. Or he really *should* like me, because I once bought him a very large plate of chicken wings. So surely there had to be some kind of mistake. Surely Adam had texted the wrong person.

Underneath my fake laughter lurked a little bit of alarm. Maybe I did look like a whale. During my mother's last year and after her death, the combination of stress and lots of restaurant food near her hospitals caused me to pack on 15 pounds. No wonder I didn't like pants. None of them fit.

It wasn't until I got home and put my kayak away that I figured the whole thing out. Adam must have texted the wrong person. He'd meant to text the Hobo and tell him that Max Garver thought *the Hobo* was a whale—not me. I've often texted one person when meaning to text another person with the same last name, so it made a lot of sense. And boys love to berate each other. Torture is their rite of passage.

I decided to text Adam to point out his mistake.

Uh, Adam—this is Dawn, Levi's mom.

And then I thought I'd tease him a little bit. It's always fun to embarrass the children.

So is Max saying I'm fat?

Ten minutes later, Adam responded.

I have no idea.

Again, I say—what the hell? What did *I have no idea* mean? His words sure didn't indicate that he understood that he'd texted his best friend's *mom* instead of his best friend, which had to be the case.

Maybe he was just too mortified to offer a meaningful response. If so, then goal: achieved because like I said—it is fun to embarrass the children.

I knew enough not to press Adam for more info; I considered myself lucky to have received any reply. After all, he is a teenage boy. They aren't known for returning texts. Ever.

Still, I thought I'd roll the dice and text my son. I knew it was a dumb, pointless exercise. But as we've established in the past few pages, sometimes my wheel is spinning but my hamster's dead.

So I sent him a screenshot of Adam's message.

Was this text supposed to go to you? Or is Adam saying I'm fat? I am so very confused.

Eventually, shockingly, I received a response.

He was just trying to make me mad.

Ah-ha. See? That message had been meant for the Hobo. *He* was the whale, according to Max. All in good fun. Boys will be boys! And kudos to Adam for giving the Hobo a heads up on the matter. *Just thought you should know.* What a pal!

Since I wasn't a whale—a gross, fat whale—anymore, my mood improved. I turned on some music, started making dinner and danced around the kitchen a little, reveling in my newfound svelteness. Maybe things weren't so bad! Maybe no one had noticed my recent weight gain!

Maybe my pants would one day fit again!

A girl could only dream.

The mastiff and the Meth Lab interrupted my reverie, barking like morons at their own family members the way they always do. The Hobo, home from school, entered the kitchen.

"Hello, Son," I said.

He walked to the coffee table and put down his backpack. "Hey, Mom."

"That was some message from Adam today," I said. "I bet he was embarrassed, texting me by accident like that!"

"Oh, he didn't do it by accident," he said. "It was meant for you."

I stopped setting the table and turned to him. "What do you mean? So Max thinks I look like a whale?"

"Yeah, that's what I already told you. Max was trying to make me mad. So he said 'Your mom's a whale.'"

Whale, shit.

Game: over. Mystery: solved. Fifty years, two fantastic kids, a great marriage, a solid career, and one relatively successful first book.

All to be reduced to a Yo Mama joke.

"Did you guys let Max know that Adam told me what he said?"

The Hobo nodded. "Yeah, and Max did say he was sorry."

I just stood there, plate frozen in midair.

Mindful of my emotions, the boy walked over and patted my back. "He was just trying to mess with me. After Adam texted you, Max felt bad and said to tell you that he thinks you're a real nice lady!"

A real nice lady I thought.

Who looks like a whale.

A gross, fat whale.

I shook my head, disbelief mixed with hilarity mixed with a deep, abiding, profound feeling.

That I would never buy Max Garver chicken wings.

Ever, ever again.

5
Here–Take My Money

You might not know it to look at me, but I am an absolute sorceress.

I have the power to change, transform and alter reality with just a snap decision, a wave of my hand and a swipe of my credit card.

Why? you ask.

Huh? you wonder.

What the hell are you talking about? you say.

I'm not kidding you–I am a magician. The most recent example of my sorcery is the fact I have turned a 99-cent goldfish into an $800 goldfish.

Now, I may be a sorceress, but I'm not a greedy sorceress. Allow me to give you some Helpful Guidance™ on how you, too, can turn a 99-cent goldfish into an $800 goldfish.

- On a nice spring morning, sit on front porch and gaze at your ornamental pond. It's a small, simple and relatively low-maintenance little pond, so you suddenly feel the need to screw it all up. You decide that small + simple + low maintenance = way too easy, so you proceed to have a really bad idea.
"I'll get some goldfish!" you say.
"It'll be fun!" you say.
- While shopping at Walmart the next day, head over to the pet department and pick out two goldfish–one orange comet fish of the ping-pong-ball-at-the-carnival variety, and one pretty white fantail of the stays-in-a-bowl-in-the-house variety. You aren't sure the fancy fantail will survive in a pond, but a quick Google search says it can, and if it's on the internet, it must be true.
- Pay 99 cents for each fish, take them home and place them in their bag in the pond for a half-hour to acclimate to water

temperature, per your instructions from the underpaid Walmart worker who received exactly four minutes of pet-care training. When the 30 minutes are up, release fish from bag into the pond. Check on them several times, feed them in the evening, and predict that they'll be just fine.

- Go out next morning and find only one living fish, the fancy white fantail. She swims around the plain orange carny fish as it floats on top of the pond, one eyeball to the heavens. Grab net and lift dead carny fish from water, then give it a proper Ty-D-Bol burial and return to pond to stare at remaining fish. Decide that the fantail, who has no emotions and exactly one brain cell, looks sad.
- Spend next several weekends trekking to Walmart and buying more 99-cent fish to keep the fantail company. The reason you have to keep buying fish is simple: They all die. Except for the fantail, who in your expert opinion, still looks terribly sad.
- After six trips to Walmart and dozens of dead 99-cent fish, figure out maybe you shouldn't buy animals from the same store you buy soup and toilet paper. Head to Petland and purchase pricier goldfish, hoping to find some healthier friends for the lonely fantail. Realize you've now spent no less than $50 in support of a goldfish's mental health.
- Upon scooping up the dead Petland goldfish the following weekend, you decide the pond could be the problem. Sure, the white fantail is still perfectly fine. But something must be wrong with the water or structure itself to wreak so much havoc in what you now call the Apocalypse Pond.
- Drive to Lowe's and spend $350 on a larger pond shell, which of course necessitates a $100 upgraded pump and filtration system. Pay excavator $150 to bring his backhoe over and install the new shell, explaining to him that you need a bigger pond because your goldfish is lonely. Watch him cry tears of laughter while digging a giant hole in your yard.
- The clean water of the upgraded pond looks wonderful, but it shows a fantail clearly mourning her fallen comrades. She hides dejectedly under the filtration system, pondering a life of meaninglessness.
- Off you go to Petland, where they now have your credit card on file and know you by your first name. Head over to fish department and decide to really splurge on two $7.99 koi fish, which you should have been buying all along because they're meant for outdoor ponds. Unlike cheap goldfish, which are

meant for bowls and, in some countries, dinner.
- Introduce the two koi to the fantail, who is still hiding under the filter. Watch over the next several weeks as the three of them eat, swim and bond—as much as animals with three combined brain cells can bond.
- As fall begins, become concerned that fish might freeze to death during winter. You Google it to find that pond fish can live through cold weather just fine, but even though it's-on-the-internet-so-it-must-be-true, you remain unconvinced. Off you go to your pals at Petland, where you drop $150 on a huge indoor aquarium, filter and heater.
- Bring it all home and listen to spouse mutter angrily upon seeing the receipt. Set up aquarium, toss your net in the trash can and use your largest mixing bowl to catch fish, who used to be 2 inches long but are now each the size of dinner plates. Put them in tank, sit back and gaze at animals that, in the past three months, have cost you as much as your first car.

And that's how you do it, folks. I said I'd share my magic with you, and I did. The preceding paragraphs describe in-depth how to turn a 99-cent goldfish into an $800 goldfish and blow a big chunk of your kid's college fund on an animal you purchased for less than a bag of potato chips.

With this valuable information, you too can be a sorceress. You, too, can be a knucklehead. No, really—no thanks are necessary. I'm always here to help.

6
I Can't See Clearly Now

Sometimes I forget I'm a geezer.

And the fact I *forget* that I am a geezer makes me even more of a geezer. But whatever.

The point is I get it in my head that I'm 25, 35–hell, even 45–and make the monumentally bad decision not to wear my glasses. This has proven to be disastrous on more than one occasion, but yet I do it all the time–walk around without my specs thinking I can still see.

Used to be I had perfect vision. In fact, somehow I had "better than perfect" vision according to a nurse who once tested my eyesight and gushed, "You have the best vision I've ever seen!" This was exciting for me, and I regularly bragged about it to the Husband, the kids and lots of other people who didn't care.

The date of that particular eye exam was December, 1997. My age at the time? Twenty-eight.

Nonetheless, the nurse's "better than perfect" diagnosis stayed with me for decades, so when my eyes started to go in my 40s I had no clue. I'd worked in the journalism and communications fields since 1992, and couldn't figure out why the text in all our agency's publications was so small all of a sudden.

"What is wrong with these editors, making the words so tiny?" I asked my co-worker Erik one day, waving a brochure at him. "This text should be at least 11 points!"

He glanced at the piece I held. "I think it is 11 points," he said, taking off his glasses. "Here–want to try my readers?"

I waved them away. "I don't need those. A nurse once told me I have the best vision she's ever seen!"

"When was that?" he asked.

"1997," I said.

Erik smiled. "So, like, 15 years and two presidents ago. You know for most people, vision starts to deteriorate in their 40s. That's when mine started to go. You sure you don't want to try these?"

He held his glasses out to me again. I decided to take them, only so I could prove to him my awesome vision. "Alright."

I put them on, lifted the brochure up to my face, and beheld something wonderful. Something beautiful. Something completely readable.

Such as words.

"Whoa!" I said.

Erik chuckled. "I know, right? When you get to be our age, readers rock!"

"Where can I buy these?" I asked. Thanks to my "better than perfect!" vision, I was completely clueless about readers.

"Just about anywhere," he said. "Walmart, the drug store—even grocery stores have them."

That was all I needed to hear. Even though I allegedly had great vision, I'd always been secretly fond of glasses and jealous of women who wore them because I think they make people look smart. I'm blonde, so most folks think I'm a nitwit. I need all the smart I can get.

So I began buying glasses at Walmart, the drug store—even at the grocery store. My favorite purchase spot became Dollar Tree, where I could load up on five or more pairs for five or more dollars. I put readers on my coffee table, side table, kitchen table—ALL the tables.

But even with readers placed here, there and everywhere, I somehow forget to actually *wear* them, and like I said earlier, forgetting things = geezer. It's also entirely possible I forget the glasses because I just can't *see* them.

It's a vicious geezer circle.

One of the worst times to forget readers, I've found, is when getting dressed. I've had several major clothing-related mishaps due to lack of glasses, including but not limited to wearing pants inside out, putting two different shoes on two different feet and cheerfully wearing a maternity shirt—all day, mind you—when I wasn't pregnant . . .

. . . and the baby was 9.

With wardrobe malfunctions like these, you'd think I'd simply wear my glasses while looking in the closet each morning. But no, I seldom do, and the cycle continues.

Just last month, I put on a top sans glasses and wore it to volunteer at an outdoor concession stand for the kids' high school. Temps were in the high 80s, but thanks to the lightweight fabric of my shirt I felt a cool gentle breeze on my skin when I stepped out of the car.

What a great blouse for summer! I thought.

I wasn't the only fan of my top. As I walked across the grass to the concession stand, I noticed lots of folks looking at it.

People really like my shirt! I thought.

I passed an old man leaning on a cane. He winked at me and smiled.

It's making everyone so happy! I thought. *I will wear this more often.*

I looked down to make a mental note of the shirt, and it was then that I saw it.

In the glaring hot sunlight of a September afternoon, there it was:

My very white bra.

Through my very red shirt.

My very sheer, apparently very see-through red shirt.

"Well, shit," I said.

Too late to go home and change, I spent the rest of the day working in the concession stand with a visible white bra under a bright red shirt. I was mortified. I was horrified.

I was just about naked.

You would think that from then on, I'd learn to wear my glasses.

You would be wrong.

Not even two weeks later, I pranced out of the house without my specs yet again for a big back-to-school sale at Kohl's. Because of said sale, the racks were a mess. But I managed to find a really cool shirt for the Hobo after a long time spent rummaging through for his size.

I was excited. The shirt featured a large PlayStation logo, so I knew the video-game obsessed Hobo would love it and give me a gratitude-filled hug and kiss. He's 16 now. There is no affection without bribery.

With that in mind, I ran to the cash register, drove home and braced myself for entirely voluntary hugs and kisses.

"Look what I got you!" I said, rushing inside to hand him the Kohl's bag.

He opened the bag and pulled out the T-shirt. "A PlayStation shirt. That's pretty cool," he said, nodding.

"Right?" I clapped my hands in glee. Voluntary hugs and kisses were surely coming my way.

He unfolded the shirt and held it up. "But it looks a little . . . " he peered at the tag. "Mom, this isn't the right size."

"Yes, it is! I spent 10 minutes digging through the rack to find you a medium," I grabbed the shirt and pointed at the tag. "See? 'M'–medium."

The Hobo shook his head. "Mom," he said, "you better put on your glasses."

"What are you talking about?" I said.

I scoffed.

I tsked.

I grabbed my readers from the kitchen table and put them on my face. And there, plain as day, was the truth:

XL

Not M, but XL.

I took my glasses off. Looked like an M.

I put my glasses on. Looked like an XL.

Because it was an XL.

"Well, shit," I said.

The Hobo laughed. "That's OK, Mom." He bent over, hugged me and kissed the top of my head.

Entirely voluntarily, I might add.

"Sometimes you forget you're a geezer."

7
Open Mouth, Insert Foot

I've been losing lots of things lately. My phone. My glasses. My mind.

It's just a part of growing older, I know because I'm losing other important items, too: my eyesight, my collagen and occasionally, my will to live.

But never in a million years did I think I'd lose this particular thing so early. I thought it'd be years, decades, maybe never before I'd ever experience such a loss.

Well, let me tell you. It happened just this week. It's over, I'm finished, the end, because . . .

I've done gone and lost my damn filter.

It's true. Along with my hair, my hearing, my muscle tone and countless other items, I appear to be losing the ability to hold my tongue and refrain from telling people what I really think. Even when I should stay quiet. Even when it'll hurt someone's feelings. Even when I look like a complete asshole. My mouth opens of its own accord and just spews forth the truth, feelings and assholes be damned.

Although I turned 50 in April, I thought I was far too young to begin telling folks what I really think. Normally an oldster loses his or her filter much later in life, say around 80 or so. It matters less then because one's friends have started dying off, and most geezers are far too crabby to make new friends anyway. So you can basically walk around blabbing anything because people figure that since you're close to death, you can do whatever you want. Diarrhea of the mouth is not as offensive to complete strangers.

Nonetheless, complete strangers are who I managed to offend the other day when my co-worker Al and I went to the cafeteria for lunch. We'd been perusing the various food offerings and stopped to admire the Mexican station.

"Mmm," said Al. "Look at that."

"I know," I said. "Chicken, guacamole . . . that looks great! I think I'm going to get a bowl, some chips . . ."

And right then, it happened. I paused, looked up at the price of the meal, then lost my damn filter.

"NINE DOLLARS!!" I yelled.

Time stood still. Silence filled the room. Food fell from mouths. Sixty-odd people inside the cafeteria stopped what they were doing to turn and look at me.

Al had disappeared, likely dissolving into the floor from sheer embarrassment. The three servers who worked the station–whose salary the nine-dollar meals paid–glared at me with intense disgust, and rightfully so.

What the hell, I could hear them thinking, *is wrong with that woman? Is she insane? On drugs? Is she just horribly rude?*

No, dear people, I thought, *I am just a total and complete cheapskate–especially when it comes to lunch.*

I'm such a horrible lunch cheapskate that I'd only recently started allowing myself to purchase a noon meal, instead of packing something inexpensive and depressing like I did for many years. I am a woman who lived on Progresso Italian-Style Wedding soup, at $1.89 per can, for nearly 18 months. I wish I could bring myself to spend more on food, but alas: I am too far gone.

See, even though I make more money than I ever have, inside I'm still a poor kid from outside Youngstown. And as I've said before, the proverbial steel mill could close at any time. So I eat inexpensive foods for lunch, foods that smack of poverty. Layoffs. Despair.

I am truly a horrible, terrible cheapskate. But there was no way to express that to the complete strangers gaping at me in the cafeteria. So I turned around and left.

In the hall, I found Al doubled over in hysterics.

"NINE DOLLARS!" he yelled, his voice echoing *DOLLARS! DOLLARS! DOLLARS!* down the narrow corridor. "I know," I said. "Shut up."

He shook his head as we walked back to the elevators. "Man, what is wrong with you? Yelling at those poor workers making minimum wage. Nine dollars is, like, two hours pay for them!"

"I know," I said. "Please–shut up."

We stepped onto the elevator and I hoped that would be the end of it.

But, no. He just couldn't stop himself. "NINE DOLLARS!" he chortled, doubling over again.

I slugged him in the arm. "Stop it! You know I only ever spend, like, $6 for lunch at the most. Nine dollars is way too much!"

He rubbed his stomach. "Mmm," he said. "I don't think about the price. If I do, my belly says 'Don't you worry about it, Al. Get that food in here.'"

There was no use arguing with him. After all, Al is a man who's been known to eat three Chipotle burritos in one day. And although he is also from Youngstown, his family wasn't poor like mine. He lived in a nice home, went to a good Catholic school . . . I mean, he owned his very own Big Wheel and didn't have to share it with anyone. Al's proverbial steel mill never closes, and if it seems like I'm a little bit jealous of his childhood, it's because I am.

The elevator doors opened, and we stepped onto the 25th floor.

"NINE DOLLARS!" he yelled, as we entered our department. "NINE DOLLARS!!"

Like gophers from holes, the rest of my co-workers' heads popped over their cubicle walls waiting for Al, a masterful storyteller, to regale them with tales of my idiocy.

It was going to be a long afternoon.

He headed off to entertain the troops as I slumped back to my desk. I sat down and realized that in my shame, I'd completely forgotten to buy anything at all to eat.

I opened my desk drawer, grabbed a can of Progresso Italian-Style Wedding Soup–$1.89–and succumbed to yet another disappointing lunch. I wondered: Would I ever change? Would I ever realize my proverbial steel mill hadn't closed? Would I ever decide I was worth a meal that cost more than a gallon of gas?

Probably not. I'd likely just continue on my dismal path. Just another short, sad, soup-sipping white woman . . .

NINE DOLLARS! . . . DOLLARS! . . . DOLLARS!

. . . who done gone and lost her damn filter.

8
I Have Issues

Needles are tools of the devil. I know this because every time I see a needle approach my skin, I faint.

Or vomit.

Or both.

Yep. I have a needle problem. Sure, lots of people say they have needle problems, but let me tell you, I have ALL the needle problems, and actually, calling it a just a problem doesn't even begin to describe the scope and magnitude of my issue.

I am afraid, terrified and disgusted by needles. The mere suggestion of getting a vaccination or a blood test makes me sweat, spikes my blood pressure and causes my heart to pound as if I'm being chased by a herd of hungry lions, all of which have hypodermic needles for teeth.

Ugh. I fucking hate needles.

I apologize. I try not to swear but such is the severity of my problem with needles. Like I said, when I'm eventually forced to get a shot or a blood draw, I either faint or puke, usually both. Doctors, nurses and phlebotomists laugh off my objections whenever they approach me with needles. I try to warn them. I try.

"I don't like needles," I tell them. "I will faint. Or vomit. Or both!"

"You'll be fine," they say, smiling. "It's just a little prick."

You never want the last words you hear to be "little prick."

Yet that's what I inevitably hear as I slide fainting to the floor, vomiting all the way.

So yes. I fucking hate needles.

Even so, I've managed to make a complete ass of myself and cause a medical emergency because of needles four times in my adult life. That's right—count 'em, four. One, two, three, four.

The earliest needle incident happened when I was fresh out of college, a young newspaper photographer in northeast Ohio. With my brand-new photojournalism degree, I had big dreams of taking award-winning photos in war-torn nations.

That did not happen. My first job out of school was as an intern at a small newspaper where I covered pet-of-the week, ribbon-cuttings and holiday decorating contests.

So many holiday decorating contests.

One freezing December afternoon, I arrived at a middle-aged woman's home in northern Trumbull County to photograph her Christmas tree, for yet another entry into yet another decor contest. She was giddy at the thought of having her displays photographed for the competition.

"Oh good, you're here! I have everything all lit up and ready to go," she said.

"Great. Thanks," I said.

My 10-billionth Christmas tree photo of the week. I could barely contain my excitement.

Ambling in, lugging my gear, I unpacked and began shooting her giant, long-needled tree. She had many suggestions for good photos.

I had some suggestions for her—and what she could do with her tree.

Even though I never said them out loud, the tree must have read my mind. As Crazy Christmas Lady dragged me around for yet another angle of her mammoth holiday monster, it happened. Her arm, in conjunction with the evil tree, pulled back a long-needled branch and whacked me full-force in the eyeball.

Ahhh! NEEDLES in my EYE! Searing pain! Blinding bright light! Did I mention the NEEDLES in my EYE?

You want Christmas? I'm pretty sure I saw Jesus that day. I know I said his name—and stuff.

Blind and gushing liquid from my eye, I tried to sit down for a minute to regain my vision.

But Crazy Christmas Lady wasn't having it. She grabbed my sleeve, pulled me up and yanked me to yet another angle of her demon tree.

I faked a couple more photos, said goodbye and left. I had to get away from that nut job before I punched her.

One eye working, the other flowing like a faucet, I somehow drove back to the newsroom. The boss took one look at my pummeled face and drove me to the hospital, where I received the happy news that NEEDLES in my EYE weren't quite going to be enough that day. The tree had scratched my cornea, so I'd need a tetanus shot.

The doctor delivering this news could only be described as McDreamy. Thick hair, chiseled face, big blue eyes—I was single at the time and I didn't see a ring on his finger. Unfortunately, I knew I had zero chance with him on account of the three coats of mascara running down my snotty, swollen face.

So I told McDreamy that I really wouldn't need a tetanus shot.

"You know, I'm immune to Christmas tree germs, so I don't think . . . " I said.

But he was adamant in his mission to poke me.

(And not in any kind of way I wanted him to poke me.)

I waited on the exam chair for 20 agonizing minutes until McDreamy and a nurse came back with the tray of NEEDLE.

"Oh! I'm gonna throw up!" I told McDreamy. (So sexy. I bet he wanted me.)

"Get her the trash can!" he said.

And then it went black.

I woke up on the floor, passed out in a little puddle of my own puke, with McDreamy waving smelling salts in my face while the nurse cleaned up my vomit. They had, at least, used my blackout as an opportunity to give me the tetanus shot. For this, I was very grateful.

Patch over my eye, prescription for drops in my pocket, I left the hospital. I healed up soon enough and decided that I'd learned a valuable life lesson from the incident–mainly how to file a workers' comp claim.

Still, needles–and Christmas trees–weren't done with me yet. No sir.

A few years later during the holidays, I was running speaker wire around the living room when I stepped on glass from a broken tree ornament. Teeny-tiny slivers of German glass poked directly through the ball of my right foot, and let me tell you–it hurt like a sum-bitch.

So I did the smart thing: ignored it. Eventually, I figured, the glass would work its way out of my foot.

For three years, I tried this "ignore" tactic. Three years of step STAB step STAB step STAB.

Those Germans can make some glass.

And still, I limped around with festering glass in my foot instead of doing anything about it because I knew I would need minor surgery sure to be filled with NEEDLE.

Step STAB. Step STAB. Step STAB. I limped and limped until I could limp no more and finally one day, I made an appointment.

Sadly, the doctor was no McDreamy. But he seemed like a nice enough man, very interested in my career.

"You're a newspaper photographer? Cool job. You're lucky," he said.

Looking at the doctor, assessing his probable $250,000 per year salary compared to my $24,000, I said nothing. I also thought it best not to mention my standard Christmas tree and ribbon-cutting assignments, hoping "Cool Job" status would keep me from his NEEDLE.

Alas. It was not to be.

Out came the tray of NEEDLE to numb my foot. Long . . . sharp . . . NEEDLE.

"Ahhhhh–that's way too big!" I said. "I don't like needles!"

"This will just numb you," he said.

It sure didn't feel that way, as he poked around my foot. The hyperventilating began, the nausea, and still, he jabbed me at least 14 times. There are more than 7,000 nerve endings in a foot. I think he hit them all.

"Owwwwww-uhhh!" I screamed.

"Photographers are supposed to be tough! It's just a little prick!" he said.

And then it went black.

When I came to, my foot was cut and bandaged, the glass was removed, and the doc stood over me as the nurse wiped, you guessed it, my vomit from the floor.

"Man," he said, shaking his head. "I thought photographers were supposed to be tough." He pulled off his gloves and walked out the door.

It was clear I'd disappointed him, just as I'd done with Doc McDreamy years before. So I once again made it my mission to avoid needles–and Christmas trees–as much as possible.

I succeeded for many years.

Until I made the horrible decision to donate blood.

Now, donating blood is not supposed to be a bad decision. There are lots of wonderful words to describe the simple act of giving blood: "selfless," "generous" and "empathetic" come to mind.

However, as you can see from the above anecdotes, words to describe *me* donating blood include "dumb," "foolish" and "an extraordinarily bad idea."

Knowing that, I still made the really stupid decision to give blood one day about five years after the foot incident. My workplace was hosting one of their many blood drives, which I normally ignore due to the threat of NEEDLE.

Unfortunately, my mother had just undergone a quadruple bypass and had been given absolute gallons of blood during her surgery and recovery, so I felt extra grateful for the donations that had helped save her. In addition, my blood type is O negative–the universal donor–so I knew my contribution would be extra valuable.

This is how I found myself walking down the hallway of the second floor of my office building to the health clinic. *Surely, you've outgrown the needle thing by now,* I thought. But there was no telling my subconscious that. My hands shook, my heart pounded and beads of sweat began collecting on my forehead.

Nonetheless, I soldiered on, full of false optimism and my very useful O negative blood.

I walked into the clinic, signed up for the blood drive, then sat down and waited. At that point, I knew there was no going back. So I began talking to myself. You know, out loud. Like a mental patient.

"You'll be fine!" I said.

"It's just a little prick!" I said.

The other four blood donors in the waiting room glanced up from their phones to look at me. I avoided their gaze, pulled out my phone, and pretended to be a sane adult instead of an insane child.

Which didn't work. With each co-worker who left the room to donate, my pulse quickened. Sweat ran down my spine and my right eye began twitching, probably recalling its own needle run-in. My legs started trembling so uncontrollably that I had to bob them up and down in front of me.

You know. Like a mental patient.

I was just about to chicken out and leave when I heard the words. The dreaded words.

"Dawn Weber?"

I stood, wobbled across the floor and into the room, where I collapsed onto the exam table in front of the nurse. "I just want you to know up front that I don't do very well with needles."

"Lots of people say that," she said, waving me off.

"No, I mean it. I have a serious issue."

She tied the rubber strip around my arm and pulled a small needle from its sheath. "Don't worry. People tell me they don't even feel anything when I draw blood. Anyway, you'll be fine. Look at this tiny needle. It's just a little prick."

Figuring a closed mouth would be the best way to block any impending vomit, I didn't say anything else. I just watched in horror as the NEEDLE approached the soft white flesh of MY ARM.

Then, I closed my eyes, held my breath and prepared to faint. Or puke.

Or both.

This time, however, something magical happened. The nurse indeed had a very gentle touch with her small needle, and I barely felt anything. Not a little prick at all, just a light pinch.

I opened my eyes and stared at her in wonder. "You *are* really good–that was nothing!"

She smiled and pulled the tourniquet off my arm. "Told you."

I thanked her, sat up and drank the juice she offered. Not only was I grateful to Nurse No-Prick, but I was also downright giddy that I'd finally given blood like a bonafide grown-up.

I walked out the door, down the hallway and into the freight elevator bay, where I promptly fainted.

I'm not sure how long I was there. The freight elevators aren't used by many people, but I'd decided to take one that day because I needed to go to my photo studio in the basement. This had turned out to be a bad idea, and I must have laid there for . . . 10 minutes? Twenty minutes? I still have no idea.

Eventually, thankfully, Wanda the cleaning lady rolled her cart into the bay and found me. She patted my arm and called my name.

"Dawn? Hey Dawn," she said. "Are you alright?"

I opened my eyes and regarded her in a dreamy haze. I'd always really liked Wanda, although I'd never been sure why. Maybe it was because she always seemed to be in a good mood. Maybe it was because she reminded me of my grandmother.

Maybe it was because I somehow knew deep down that one day, she'd find me passed out on the floor.

She was, it seemed, my freight-elevator angel.

"I guess so," I said, rubbing my forehead. "I must've fainted after I gave blood. I think I hit my head, too."

Wanda grabbed her two-way radio and called the employee health center. Nurse No-Prick rushed out of the blood drive to the elevators, and she and Wanda sat me up slowly, gave me packs of ice for my head and generally made a big, embarrassing fuss.

"Wow," Nurse No-Prick said. "You really do have a phobia."

"It's OK, I'm OK," I said, horrified that I'd once again made an idiot of myself over a damn needle.

A security guard arrived in the bay with a wheelchair, helped me into it and wheeled me back to the health clinic where the nurse put me in a hospital bed and called my department. My co-workers texted. My boss came to check on me. I tried to get up and go back to work, but No-Prick shooed me back into bed.

"You need to stay for at least an hour this time so we can make sure you're stable," she said.

One hour. Plenty of time to fill out the three-page long incident report and sit and think about the fact that I'd caused a three-alarm medical emergency because of a needle the length of a child's fingernail.

I finished the paperwork and twiddled my thumbs. By the time the 60 minutes were up, I felt pretty good aside from a sore head. So with No-Prick's permission, I arose from the bed, walked out the door and made my way to the deserted elevators again, where there was no Wanda, no freight-elevator angel, to save me.

While waiting to ride to the basement, I stared at the floor tiles–the ones I'd so recently laid upon–and decided that even though I'd again passed out because of a needle the width of a strand of hair, I had something to be grateful for. It was definitely good news, so wonderful that I decided to say it out loud–to no one.

You know. Like a mental patient.
"Well," I said, "at least I didn't puke."
Then, from my battered head came the throbbing voice of reason.
This time.

9
Hello Kitty

Most cars take Turtle Wax.

My car, on the other hand, needs a bikini wax.

That's because the roof is entirely covered in pussycat hair thanks to our two evil, shedding felines. Big mounds of pussycat hair. My love, my baby, my little convertible's roof is covered in GIANT GOBS OF PUSSYCAT HAIR.

They've made it their personal landing strip.

I'm sorry. I told vulgar pussycat hair jokes, didn't I? They were too hard to resist. Also, my cats have made me mad, and when I get mad, I don't get even–I get vulgar. So brace yourself, because I'm really mad.

See, cat hair on a canvas roof is like Velcro stuck to, well, Velcro, and it does not come off, even on the interstate at 80 mph. I've tried vacuuming it, scrubbing it and sweeping it with a broom, all to no avail. About the only thing that works is picking the individual hairs off with my fingernails, one by one by freaking one.

In addition, the sheer weight of two cats on the soft top makes an indented hole where they lie, and causes a big old cat crater, damaging the roof and raising my blood pressure.

I tell them to get off. But do you think they listen? They don't, at all. Like, ever. Each day, they perch on top of my sweet, sensitive little ragtop, licking themselves and shedding, shedding, shedding.

I know this is a first-world problem, as in *Aw. The chubby American lady is sad because her convertible has cat hair on it.* I get it. With the horrors of poverty, global warming and racial unrest, we have much bigger things to worry about.

But still, important issues? You're in the wrong book.

This is mostly a book about bad ideas, and trust me, there's a really bad idea coming very soon. Plus, if it makes you feel any better, please recall from other chapters that I used to be broke as hell. It took me decades, absolute centuries, I tell you, to save for this little 15-year-old convertible. You know, the one with the ancient, fragile roof.

The roof with the cats on it.

I try to catch them in the act of jumping up there. I'm seldom successful, but when I do manage to find them launching themselves onto my car's delicate ragtop and the aging, complicated lifting mechanism underneath, I nearly vomit because getting a convertible roof repaired is expensive. And these aren't just sweet little petite pussycats. These cats are big. Very big.

Weighing in at an impressive 15 pounds is the black cat, whom we named Jet as in "jet black" because we are creative like that. She is a street-fightin', mouse-catchin', bird-slashin' solid chunk of sinew, a sneaky she-devil capable of scaring coyotes away.

Hell–sometimes she scares me away.

Then there's Willie, and let me tell you, Willie isn't just any cat–he's a large cat. He's a huge cat. He's a very, very fat cat.

Willie is gray, tabby-striped and enormous. When I take him to the vet, I never find out what he weighs because 1) I'm too afraid to ask, and 2) I usually pass out from carrying him into the office. If I had to guess, I'd say it's close to 20 pounds, maybe more, all thanks to his strenuous hobbies of eating, sleeping and parking his fat ass on the roof of my car.

If we add Jet's 15 pounds to Willie's 20 or God-knows-how much, we come up with 35-plus pounds. When the two of them launch those combined 35-plus pounds from the garage floor to the roof of my car, you'd multiply their mass times velocity times the height, and come up with a completely wrong answer because that is math, and I don't know what the hell I'm talking about.

Getting back to my point, every day those two land like bombs on my creaky old roof. There, they curl up, lie down and commence shedding in the giant hole they've created. It's in this position I usually catch them.

"Get off," I say, glaring at them from the garage doorway.

Four green eyes open and regard me, unimpressed. So I step into the garage, grumbling.

"Get off!" I yell.

Jet yawns, Willie twitches his tail, but neither one of them moves a muscle.

I proceed to lose my shit.

"GET OFF MY CAR!! HISSSSSSS!" I shriek, running at the car.

You would think, at this point, that they'd get scared. You would think they'd jump off.

You would be wrong.

As the short, chubby white woman lunges at them screaming, the cats stand, stretch languidly and walk to the other side of the rooftop, where the short, chubby white woman can't reach them. When said woman runs to the other side to catch them, you can guess what happens, and yes, you're right–they walk back to their first spot.

I have heard you can teach a cat anything. It's true, you can teach a cat anything–that *it* wants to do *on its own*. While dogs will–usually, anyway–eventually do what *you* want, cats do what *they* want, when *they* damn well want to do it.

That's because, in ancient times, cats were worshipped as gods. As far as they're concerned, nothing has changed, and they couldn't care less what you think. Honey badger don't care? Well, cats don't give a fuck.

Absolutely zero fucks given.

Knowing all this, I decided I'd never be able to actually train the cats to stay off the convertible. The only way to keep them off was to make sitting on my convertible very unpleasant.

Enter the blue tarp.

I unfolded a slippery, crunchy blue tarp and flung it over the entire car. Surely, I thought, the Furball Fairies would hate the tarp's crunchy noise as they moved around the roof. Surely prudent pusses would dislike the slick, shifty plastic.

Ha ha ha! Oh, I was so innocent then.

The tarp wasn't on three hours before both of them were planted smack-dab in the usual spot, pushing their usual cat-crater down into the car's interior. They stared at me with a look that said, *We are somewhat less comfortable, but we really enjoy your fury.*

So, no, the tarp didn't work. It was as ineffective at deterring the cats as it was from keeping their fur from the roof. I'd have to find something else.

Remember how I promised you another bad idea in this chapter? Well, enter the same blue tarp from earlier–with mothballs glued on top.

Yes, after reading that cats dislike mothballs, in my infinite wisdom I painstakingly super-glued dozens of them to the blue tarp and threw it back over the car. The glue combined with the mothballs swiftly produced a fume I like to call "Methyl-Ethyl-Deathyl-ate," or "Ethel" for short, because it smelled like old ladies.

And death.

Ethel the Toxic Cloud seeped her way from the garage to the sunroom to the kitchen to the whole house, and made every single one of us ill. I felt like my throat was closing. The Hobo, the Husband and the Princess had headaches. The dogs stumbled around, dazed, confused and even dumber than usual.

Speaking of dumb, it took me several days to realize that the fumes were from Ethel and the Mothball Tarp, but I eventually pulled it off the car and dragged it to the trash can, gagging all the while. On the way back through the garage, guess who I passed? That's right–the Fuzzball Farts, already back on the rooftop staring at me and laughing, laughing.

Jerks.

I stomped back into the house, plotting my revenge. The squirt gun and the spray bottle weren't going to cut it this time. Number One, neither was sufficient to express my level of fury, and Number Two, I'd tried them both before and they didn't work.

Nothing worked.

Next, I glanced around the kitchen, scanning the pots, pans and knives. Although I seriously considered it, I really didn't want to throw heavy, dangerous objects at the cats. After all, doing that would damage the car.

I kept searching, opening closet doors and junk drawers and even checking the refrigerator until I found just the thing. The most wonderful, perfect thing.

A thing called the scrub bucket.

This I carried to the bathroom tub where I filled it with ice-cold water. I then lugged it through the house, laughing all the way to the garage door, where I stopped and beheld the cats still perched blissfully atop my car.

"Hello, kitties," I said.

Willie twitched his tail.

"How are you this fine day?"

Jet yawned.

"I've got something for you . . ."

Neither one of them moved a muscle.

I hoisted the bucket and positioned it near my right shoulder. Then, I pivoted back and heaved it forward as hard as I could, launching three gallons of water onto the car, the cats, and mostly, myself.

"GET OFFF MY CARRRRR!" I screamed. I growled. I downright scrowled.

Finally, FINALLY, it happened. Off they shot like a rocket, to the garage floor and then straight out the door.

"AND STAY OFF!"

I marched triumphantly back into the house, dripping all the way. I put the bucket down and smiled despite my sopping wet clothes.

That'll teach them, I thought. *Now they'll stay off.*

Ha ha ha! Oh, I was so innocent then.

Tell me, do you think the scrub bucket was the answer? Do you think the ice-cold water deterred them? Do you think the Pussycat Pricks finally stayed off the car?

Of course not!

That would be far too easy and fortunate for me. I have what I like to call "Weber's Luck." If you don't know what that is, just replace the word "Weber's" with the word "Horrible," and you'll understand.

No, of course the bucket of water didn't work, and 90 minutes later when I went to the garage to check, the Furry Fuckers were back on the car glaring at me with a look that said *We hate water, but we overlooked it because we also hate you.*

It's been a few weeks since the scrub bucket incident. But today, after catching them yet again on my car, I decided to sit here on the dog-hair covered couch and Google around for more ideas. I see lots of suggestions, but guess what: cat repellent? Tried it. Cayenne pepper? Tried it. Essential oils? Sure. Let's make the experience even nicer for them. Perhaps some lavender for kitties' sounder sleep.

Disgusted with my lack of discoveries, I thumb over to Amazon and poke around. I begin typing "pet deterrent" into the search bar, and before I even get to the first r, *pet deterrent motion-activated* pops up. Motion-activated. Yes! Say what you want about Amazon, but I love it, so sue me. If Amazon doesn't have it, you don't need it. Just don't drink and Prime.

I got sidetracked by shopping, didn't I? That happens. So often.

Anyway, I refocus on the task at hand, and scroll down to see exactly what motion-activated pet deterrents Amazon offers. The PetSafe Scatmat, the Tattle Tale Sonic Training Alarm, the Sofa Scram Sonic Deterrent–all look super promising, but unfortunately, all are $55 and up. Cheapskate that I am, none of these items fit into my budget of, oh, $19.99 or less.

What to do, what to do? Think, think, think. Motion . . . deterrent . . . car . . .

Alarm.

That's it! That's what I need–some kind of motion-activated alarm I could put on the roof of the convertible. I type motion, alarm, cheap into the search bar, wait a few seconds and boom! There it is. GE Personal Security Motion-Sensing Alarm, batteries not included. One hundred twenty decibels. Fifteen dollars and fifty-two cents.

Add to cart. Add to cart RIGHT NOW.

When I get this little gizmo in two days or less, I shall affix it somehow on the roof of my car. I'll have to attach it to a box or something to keep it upright or rig it in some way, but–Ethel the Toxic Death Cloud aside–do not underestimate my MacGyver skills. As I've said, I was once poor.

Poverty: always educational.

Yes indeed, I've gone high-tech on their asses. This is no box o' mothballs. Actual coin was spent on this fine $15 GE appliance.

(Dr. Evil voice) With infrared LASER beam!

And when those two decide it's hair-hammock time, the LASER beam will sense their motion, emit an ear-splitting 120-decibel alarm, and the Fuzz-Festers will flee the crime scene.

I have high hopes for this technology. It better work.

Because the Husband is not a fan of the cats. He's not afraid of using pots, pans, knives—or bullets—and he frequently volunteers to get rid of their Hairy Highnesses. I sure don't want that to happen.

Yet.

10
Dogs With Jobs

It's a warm summer morning here in beautiful downtown Brownsville. I sit on the porch, phone and coffee in hand, and ponder two of my worst ideas:

The mastiff and the Meth Lab.

They hover near my feet, busily engaged in their favorite pastime. Every day the dogs dedicate a great chunk of time to this mission, trotting and jumping and climbing and doing it all again for hours, or as long as my nerves can stand it.

What is it, you ask? Playing ball? Eating treats? Burying steak bones?

Nope, none of that. The purpose of their exercise, their enterprise, indeed–their very lives, is . . .

Picking apples.

And after they pick the apples, these two dimwits *eat* the apples.

Yeah, you read that right. My dogs–I repeat, dogs–spend most of their late summer and fall mornings running back and forth between the front porch and the apple tree in the yard picking and eating apples, like a couple of deer or monkeys or . . . I don't know. Anything but dogs.

Fucking apples, man. Dogs picking and eating apples. I've never heard of such a thing, and I really don't know what's wrong with them. I mean, it's not like we don't feed them. They get plenty of dog food and, con-artists that they are, also manage to beg tons of table scraps from our plates. I have no idea why they want apples–most of them rotten and infested with bugs–so very badly.

Oh, but want them they do! You will never see such zeal, such dedication, such commitment, such outright enthusiasm as you will each morning when the mastiff and the Meth Lab spy the apples. Why it's as if the tree was hung with Milk Bones! With squirrels! With juicy rib eye steaks!

However, that's not the case. This thing is an ancient, half-dead fruit tree that we don't take care of, filled with dubious nasty apples that we would never eat.

Part of me isn't surprised these two knuckleheads eat our gross apples. Dogs didn't come this far in the evolutionary scheme of things by worrying about what they put in their mouths. I mean, these are animals that will happily eat their own poo. They ain't picky.

Though the mastiff and the Meth Lab both enjoy picking and eating apples like a couple of monkeys, each dog has her own distinctive method. Crackhead that she is, the Meth Lab procures her fruit in a frantic, chaotic manner, and woe to the creature caught between her and the apple tree. Her picking procedure goes like this:

1. Step onto porch. Spy apple tree.
2. Completely forget that said tree existed before.
3. Proceed to lose your shit.
4. Scramble off porch, knocking over humans, animals, SUVs–anything in your path on way to tree.
5. Arrive at tree and begin jumping like a lunatic, pulling down branches in attempt to knock apples to the ground.
6. Eventually, knock down an insect-infested apple or two. Grab one, then with the glee of a child on Christmas morning, race to porch and consume noisily at female owner's feet.
7. Finish apple, spy apple tree, forget that said tree existed before. Proceed to lose your shit. Repeat entire production.

Because she's the size of the Goodyear blimp, the mastiff relies on an entirely different fruit-picking process. Like I said, she mostly just lies around, probably due to the fact that it requires a concerted effort to hoist her gigantic body off the ground. She needs a lot of motivation to get up. But guess what will do it? Slimy rotten apples, that's what! Here's how Missy the Mastiff gets her morning snack:

1. Hear a noise, and lift head from 66th nap of the day. Notice Meth Lab staring into the front yard and losing her shit.
2. Watch Meth Lab launch herself from porch. Think to self, *Something is up with that idiot. I must investigate. Slowly.*
3. Moan, groan and whine while lifting giant rear from porch. Repeat moans, groans and whines while loping down steps into yard.
4. Trot at leisurely pace to tree, where Meth Lab is jumping like a moron in her attempt to knock down apples.
5. Eventually, see apple fall. Observe that Meth Lab is still jumping like a moron and didn't notice the apple fall. This works in your favor.
6. Pick up unnoticed apple that Meth Lab knocked down.

7. Return at leisurely pace back to porch. Moan, groan and whine while climbing steps.
8. Consume apple noisily at female owner's feet. Savor each worm and pocket of rot. Watch as Meth Lab finally realizes she's knocked down another apple and can return to porch to eat.
9. See Meth Lab eat her apple. Wait for her to finish so she can pick more for you.

There you have it, the methods by which two dogs—I repeat, dogs—get their gross, disgusting apples. Two very different techniques, sure, but both very effective as a means to an end.

And now that I think about it, each method makes sense for each dog.

For example, the Meth Lab lives life as if it's one big emergency. Don't let her petite frame, gentle brown eyes and soft black fur fool you; she's a tightly packed bundle of muscle capable of serious injury to humans, animals, dump trucks—anything in her path. An absolute whirling dervish of a dog who throws her heart, soul, teeth, claws and entire body mass into all her actions. Everything she does, she does in a frenzy. She runs. She jumps. She scratches.

You bleed.

The mastiff, on the other hand, is a completely different animal. As I've mentioned, she is a ONE HUNDRED FIFTY-FOUR POUND DOG and moves just about as quickly as you'd think a ONE HUNDRED FIFTY-FOUR POUND DOG would move, which is to say at the speed of a glacier. Life for the mastiff is something to observe in a relaxed manner, lying down at her mistress's feet, preferably chewing on a nice rotten apple.

Again, I say—fucking apples, man. I'd love to keep expounding upon the stupidity of these two fruit-pickers, but you know what?

I'm starting to realize that maybe they're not dumb.

Think about it: The Meth Lab saw a plentiful food source, albeit a nasty, bug-ridden, completely inappropriate food source, and learned how to procure it.

The big dog might also be more intelligent than I initially thought. After all, she's smart enough to wait while the Meth Lab jumps like a lunatic to pull branches and knock down apples, all so she can swipe them before the little dog realizes it.

So maybe—just maybe—I should be proud of owning the world's only apple-picking dogs, because the more I think about it, the more I think they're actually both quite brilliant. Nope, they're not stupid at all.

Just monumentally weird.

11
Breaking Bad: the Meth Lab Speaks

Even though the dogs are messy, smelly, giant pains in the ass, I know it's unfair to tell only my side of the story. So I've asked Suzie the Meth Lab to take a break from picking apples and being bad to defend herself. Read on:

Suzie not know what Woman talking about. Suzie very good dog.

Suzie also dislike "Meth Lab" classification. Suzie not smoke crystal meth, or even crack, and although Suzie try weed once, she not inhale. Anyway, Suzie don't think she is Meth Lab. Suzie believe she come from impressive bloodline of *black* Lab. And greyhound. And whippet. Possibly beagle. Maybe shepherd. Definitely pit bull . . .

Ahem.

Point is, Suzie have diverse array of relatives in tri-county area, all with formidable skills in couch-shredding, leg-humping and crotch-sniffing arena. Do Woman's kin-folk possess these talents? Suzie think not. Woman should watch mouth. Suzie have "Family." Family with teeth.

Anyway, Suzie classy dog, with very advanced palate. She always willing to try new things. Most recently, she discover tree in yard with many, many red foods high up in branches. At first Suzie unable to reach, but soon she figure out way to jump up, knock down reds and eat. Reds delicious, and Suzie can tell they contain bonus nutrition thanks to squirmy creatures inside.

Suzie extremely proud of this skill. She like to take reds to Woman on porch, but Woman never say thank you. She say, "Dogs aren't supposed to eat apples, you dummy!" Nevertheless, Suzie eat. Who she to turn down free food?

Sometimes, Man get box of dry, dusty treats for Suzie, but is not necessary, when cat box in particular offer many juicy, absolutely free treats for taking. Suzie eat anything: trees, rocks, reds, road-kill, cat poop. Where Peoples say, "Gross!" Suzie say, "Breakfast!"

Speaking of cat, why Suzie can't chase? Gray Cat run, Suzie pursue–is law of jungle passed down for millenniums. Gray Cat think he better than dog, with his yummier food, cushier bed and litter box of juicy treats. He need taken down a notch, and Suzie just dog for job.

Sometimes, Suzie get tired from her many tasks, so she take nice nap on bed. Peoples confused about Suzie bed, always calling it "damn couch" as in "Get off the damn couch!" Suzie not know why. Damn couch white, Suzie black. Since black better color, Suzie just being helpful by painting it with furs. Still, Peoples yell, and then sit on Suzie bed! Who they think they are?

Suzie smart dog, and she find way to get last laugh. See, as soon as Peoples sit on bed/damn couch, Suzie decide she need to go outside. Then Peoples must get up and open door. Next, Suzie run outside, wait two minutes till Peoples sit down again, and bark to come back in. Ha ha! Oh, Suzie enjoy this. She genius, for sure.

Suzie also like to accompany Peoples to bathroom, and sit in front of them as they deposit liquid into Suzie's Other Water Bowl. She express gratitude to Peoples with lick on face, but she always get "Stop it!" yells. Suzie not know why. She just thankful for bowl fills. And Suzie really enjoy being at eye-level with Peoples, so she make happen. Just like when she give trademark jump-up greeting to visitors. Woman always yell, "Get Down!" But human stand up, Suzie stand up. Is simple physics.

Suzie is sorry, however, about incident with old man at vet's office. Wrinkled one not expect signature Suzie "Get Down!" move. Suzie claws did scratch Wrinkle's legs, is true, but how she to know old Peoples have thin skin and take blood-thinning medication? Suzie hope Wrinkles stop bleeding someday.

Suzie also regret Big Stick incident. Suzie not realize that when she spin with seven-foot stick in mouth near Woman, giant stick blow out Woman's knees and knock her to ground. Suzie know many words–"Bad!" "No!" "Bacon!" But Woman scream words Suzie not hear before, words that sound like "duck." Suzie then try to lick face as Woman roll on ground. She obviously angry, but also partly at fault here, as she the one said, "Let's play stick!" So Suzie search yard and grab biggest stick available. If Woman want stick, Woman get small tree. Suzie is giver.

Suzie practice bark often. Best time to practice 3 a.m., while Woman, Man and Small Peoples sleep. Takes a while for them to wake up, walk out and shout, "Shut Up!" and Suzie able to enjoy many minutes of vicious barks before yells start. Suzie don't always bark in middle of night, but when she do, is for no real reason.

Suzie is serious guardian. However, despite Suzie skill, Peoples recently bring home giant animal who *also* think she guardian. At first, Suzie not sure what creature be—deer, bear, possible pony?—but soon, it bark and Suzie find out creature not deer/bear/pony, but some kind of gigantic moose/dog.

This moose/dog bark *way* more than Suzie. Show off! Suzie solve problem by tripling bark output. Now, whenever moose/dog bark, Suzie bark more, too. She won't be outdone.

Even though she avid barker, moose/dog also love to sleep. She sleep morning, afternoon and all night. Suzie feel she sleep way too much, so she help keep moose/dog awake by poking her in ribs.

But, as usual, Peoples not appreciate assistance. They yell, "Stop poking her! Go lie down!" Suzie do what they say and lie down, but then they yell, "Get off the damn couch!" Suzie just can't win.

You can see that Suzie get many yells. Woman especially enjoy yelling, and Suzie not know why—she just doing her jobs.

Woman's loudest yells come when Suzie conduct crotch-check on Peoples. Without good sniff of nethers, how else Suzie to know quality of creature before her? Humans funny animals, Suzie think, blessed with dizzying variety of pungent genitalia, yet seemingly no desire to sniff each other. Is sad, and not very smart.

You know, Suzie may be Meth Lab. But she clearly superior species.

12
Missy the Mastiff Finds Jesus

It's not easy to kill a dog the size of a Toyota Camry, but I almost did just that.

By taking her for a walk.

See, we thought Missy the Mastiff was huge because, well, she's a mastiff.

Turns out she's just plain out of shape; we just didn't know it at first. As I said, we inherited her from my mother who inherited her from someone else, so it's not like she came with an instruction manual. I had to research English mastiffs, and I read on the internet (so it must be true) that some of them can weigh up to 300 pounds. Even though she was enormous, at 154 pounds Missy was svelte for her breed—or so said the internet.

She was so svelte, in fact, that the Husband worried about her.

"Do you think I'm feeding her enough?" he asked, pointing to ridges on her sides. "I mean, it looks like you can see her ribs."

I saw the ridges, but I wasn't worried. "She's fine. She's right in the middle of her weight class."

He remained unconvinced. "But she doesn't move around very much," he said. "Maybe she's not getting enough calories."

"She walks back and forth to the apple tree," I said, shrugging. "She's just well-behaved. You're used to the Meth Lab acting like a nitwit. Anyway, Missy goes to the vet next week–they'll tell us if something's wrong."

I thought about this conversation the following Friday while waiting with Missy at the animal hospital. She'd been good for the vet tech, unlike the Meth Lab whose visits involve chaos, bloodshed, and sometimes, the police.

Missy, on the other hand, lay quietly on the floor as the tech finished her preliminary exam. "She sure is calm," she said, patting Missy's massive back. "The doctor will be in shortly."

The tech left the room, and I leaned my head against the wall as Missy snoozed. I'd forgotten what it was like to have a good dog. I felt relaxed, almost enjoying this peaceful Meth Lab-free veterinary appointment, with no chaos or police involvement whatsoever.

Interrupting my reverie, the vet knocked and opened the door. "Hi there! How's Missy today?"

"She's fine," I said. "Just needs her shots and a checkup."

The vet nodded. She picked up Missy's chart, scanned it, then stopped short.

"I see she weighs 154 pounds," she said, peering up at me from the chart. "That's too much."

I was shocked. "Really? My husband thinks he's not feeding her enough. Look–you can see her ribs!"

She rubbed Missy's sides. "Those aren't ribs. Those are fat rolls."

"But I read on the internet that mastiffs can weigh 300 pounds," I said.

"The internet," she said, snorting. "Anyway, it's not just her weight. She's out of shape. See how she's just lying there?"

I stared down at Missy. "I thought she was just a good dog. I haven't had one in so long."

"She is a good dog, but she's also unfit. She should at least be sitting up and interacting with me."

I frowned.

"Don't worry," she said. "Just give her a little less food, and take her on one extra leashed walk every day."

At that, it was my turn to snort. The vet appeared young, obviously new and not used to the rural clientele she served. There are exceptions, but most country folks don't really "leash-walk" their dogs. Our idea of a walk is opening the door and saying, "Get on out there, dog."

I wondered if Missy's age could be the culprit. She slept at least ten hours a day, and although I had no idea of her age, she appeared to be about 100 in dog years.

"How old do you think she is?" I asked.

She pulled Missy's dripping jowls back and inspected her teeth. "Well," she said. "I'd say 5 at the most."

Wow. So Missy wasn't a good *old* dog. She was a young, *fat* dog.

The vet and I coaxed Missy into a sitting position for her shots and the rest of her physical. I received no more bad news about Missy's health, but I did get another "leashed walk" lecture. I paid the bill and left with my big, fat, shockingly young dog.

Now, I pride myself on being a decent pet owner, so the vet's words bothered me and I vowed to make Missy's health more of a priority. The next day, instead of being a hillbilly and shooing her out the door, I would take her on a "leashed walk."

Sunshine! Fresh air! Red leash! Really, what could go wrong?

Ha. Have you met me? *Everything* would go wrong.

Saturday morning dawned bright and blue. I finished my coffee, gathered Missy's leash and walked to her bed in the sunroom.

"You ready?" I asked. "We're going for a walk!"

She stared at me.

"Come on, girl. Let's go!"

She didn't move.

"Missy," I said, clipping the leash to her collar. "Get up!"

She groaned.

I pulled and cajoled, then pulled and cajoled some more until she sighed and hoisted her giant rear up, down the steps and out the door with me. We climbed into the SUV and headed off to the park.

Because Missy was new to this whole walking thing, I took her to a local nature preserve that featured flat, grassy trails. I parked the car, grabbed my water bottle and opened the hatch, where she lay sprawled across the entire rear end of the vehicle.

"Okay, here we are!" I said, grabbing her leash.

She stared at me.

"This will be easy," I said. "It's totally flat."

She didn't move.

"Missy," I hissed. "Get up!"

She groaned.

The SUV shuddered as she lifted her tremendous bulk and jumped to the ground. My knees buckled. The earth cracked.

Birds fell from the sky.

But that was OK because we were finally going for our walk. Just a quick 30-minute stroll across flat, grassy terrain; a few outings like this and Missy would be in shape in no time. *It'll be easy*, I thought. "No problem!" I said.

9:08 a.m.: We began at the trail's head by strolling at a reasonable speed, Missy right at my side. This was a nice change of pace from the Meth Lab, who regularly dislocates my shoulders while dragging me across gravel parking lots. On my stomach.

9:10 a.m.: Still walking, I noticed Missy lagging behind a bit. *What a good girl!* I thought. *She's letting me lead!*

9:15 a.m.: Heading around a bend, I felt the leash pull me from behind. I turned to find Missy slowing her steps. "Come on, girl!" I said. "You can do it!"

9:18 a.m.: I was yanked to a halt at the end of the leash, so I looked behind me. Missy had stopped. Missy lay down.

Missy was done.

Not only done, but completely spent and flat on her side in the grass. She panted. She slobbered. She stared at the horizon as if she saw Jesus.

I ran to her side. "Missy!"

She didn't move.

I knelt down and petted her ribs/fat rolls. "Are you OK?"

She stared into the distance, still looking for the Lord.

"Jesus! I think I killed you!"

She groaned.

A 10-minute walk. That was all it took to nearly kill a dog as big as a refrigerator. I unscrewed the lid of my water bottle, which was just barely big enough for her giant tongue.

"Drink this."

She ignored me at first but eventually raised her head enough to take a few slurps. I sat beside her in the grass for a good 20 minutes until she cooled down and had the strength to get up. We limped to the parking lot, where I had the fun and glamorous task of lifting a dog that weighed more than me into my vehicle.

I wish I could say Missy recovered as soon as I got home, but she slept, limped and otherwise moped around in pain for several days. On the fourth day–just as I was about to make another call to the vet–she resumed walking normally.

It was probably a good thing I didn't call. I'd just get another lecture, even though taking Missy for a walk had been a terrible idea. Judging by her near-death experience, Missy is clearly not up for any kind of sustained exercise. She can barely handle her 12-second walks to the apple tree.

And that's ok. Hey–she may not be a good *old* dog, but she is great at being a good, young, really *fat* dog.

Leashed walk my ass.

13
Missy the Mastiff Speaks

Not to be outdone by the Meth Lab a couple chapters back, Missy the Mastiff set aside her strenuous jobs of sleeping, drooling and smashing everyone's feet to tell her enormous side of the story. Read on.

Missy know she big. Missy can't help. She born like this.

Still, Woman always say Missy "Too big!" Woman also always say "Move!" "Ouch!" "Go Away!" Missy seem to forever be in Woman's way, but she just trying to help.

For example, when Woman in kitchen, she clumsy and drop many foods on floor. Missy could be sleeping, but instead she choose to assist Woman by sitting right beside her and catching foods before they fall to ground. Sometimes, true to her name, Missy misses. Is OK. If crumbs reach floor, she make quick work of licking up. Missy don't like to brag, but she very useful.

But what thanks do Missy get for this? She get no thanks, only yells. "You tripped me!" "Go lie down!" "You're way too big!" among many things Woman shout. So Missy do her cleaning quick-like before Woman realize Missy there. When Woman stumble and fall over Missy, yells start, and Missy must go lie down and wait for next time.

Missy don't really mind lying down. Sleeping her main hobby anyway, aside from helping Woman in kitchen. Missy pride self on napping five, six, seven hours a day, then eight, nine, ten hours at night. Is gift, to be able to sleep so much, and necessary for Missy health. Big dog need big sleep.

Even in deep sleep, Missy also help by waking up to give lots of barks. See, since Missy ears big, she hear more noises. Planes in sky, leaves on driveway, feathers on floor—Peoples can't hear, so Missy say "WOOF!"

Missy also give barks when each of her Peoples come home. Missy not stupid; she recognize family. Missy just like to keep everyone informed.

When Missy come to live here at new house, she notice Meth Lab not very good informer. She not give nearly enough barks. So Missy teach Meth Lab to bark more often because Missy is generous. This took time–Meth Lab dumb as box of rocks and twice as bad, but eventually she copy Missy barking technique. And now, even though she stupid, Meth Lab bark and bark. Missy very proud.

Peoples need both of us. They can use all help they can get, as they oblivious to important events. Wind blow, rain fall, ant crawl on porch–Missy and Meth Lab alert Peoples to all of this and more with many barks because they serious protectors. Missy especially like to alert Peoples when she hear howls at night. She say, "AHHH-OOOOO!" right back, then Peoples say, "It's just a siren!" and give more yells. Must be crime to howl, but Missy can't see why.

Speaking of crime, one time Woman try to kill Missy by forcing her to go for thing called "walk." Missy try to indicate to Woman she tired–she not up for "walk." But Woman tug and pull at rope on Missy's collar, and Missy have no choice.

Woman drive Missy to grass-place, then pull rope and collar once more. Missy try again to tell Woman she not up for walk, but Woman insist, so Missy jump from car to ground and cause small earthquake.

Then Woman begin walking fast. Missy alarmed–she worry maybe someone chase Woman, but when Missy look back, she see nobody. Woman walk fast for no good reason and pull Missy hard by rope and collar. Missy try, but she can't keep up, and soon, Missy get hot. Missy pant.

Missy fall down.

She don't remember much of next few minutes. She recall seeing shape of Jesus in sky, and think maybe He will end her misery. She hear Woman shout "Missy! Jesus!" over and over. Missy think, Y*es, Woman–He right over there.*

Finally, Missy eyes clear, and she lift head to get drink from Woman. Missy OK eventually, but this close call. Hopefully, Woman not try "walk" with Missy again.

Meth Lab, on other hand, that dog could use walk, or at least large dose of Valium. She have way too much energy. She nothing but constant black blur, running rings around Missy as Missy try to rest. Meth Lab never need sleep, and she seem to get great joy from keeping Missy awake.

But don't worry–Missy get revenge. Every day, Meth Lab go outside, jump up and pull down branches to shake red foods from tree so she can eat. But thanks to fact that she spastic moron, she often not realize when they fall. So Missy steal reds right out from under her. She genius like that.

Smart as she be, Missy sometimes miscalculate things like head, chest, butt, etc. Missy seem to especially have problem with paws. People feet seem to always be underneath Missy paws. Missy go this way, step on feet. Missy go that way, step on other feet. She get lots of foot-yells, no matter how she try. So she go lie down, and look sad.

In fact, Missy look sad always, even when she happy. This work to Missy advantage, because Peoples want to cheer her up with treats, bones and belly rubs, of which Missy is big fan. So she make sure to look extra sad most of time, especially around Woman, who seem to be deeply in tune with Missy "sad" face. Woman hand out more treats, bones and belly rubs than all other Peoples combined.

Yes, despite fact Woman give many yells and one time almost kill Missy, she nice. Of Peoples in house, she pet Missy most of all.

Missy also know somehow that if not for Woman, she have no home. So Missy give Woman lots of licks, even though Woman say "Ew!" "Yuck!" and "You drool too much!"

Still, Woman know Missy can't help. She born like this.

14
Bacon Envy

He stares out the window, transfixed.

Mouth open, jaw dropped, stock still–the Husband is frozen by fascination. I mean, he's dumbstruck. He's spellbound. He is downright drooling.

What has captivated him so? A fancy car? A Harley Davidson? A beautiful, sexy woman? Aside from me, that is?

I kid, I kid. I make a joke.

The truth is he's staring at none of the above. The object that has caught the Husband's eye, glued him to the window and stopped him dead in his tracks is . . .

. . . bacon.

Someone else's bacon, at that. Specifically, the neighbor's bacon. He is drooling over another man's bacon.

We're camping at Hocking Hills Ohio in our toasty, cozy, entirely bacon-free camper. I'm not at the window with him; I'm sitting at the table, thinking how nice it is to be warm and comfortable because for years we were rustic campers. Or as I've always called it, stupid campers.

Back in the day the Husband and I used to fancy ourselves quite the rustic campers, otherwise known as dummies. To that end, we purchased one piece of camping gear together–a sleeping bag built for two. Tent? We didn't need no stinkin' tent. We were the original John and Yoko granola hippies. Getting back to nature and whatnot.

But after too many trips to putrid, horrifying outhouses–and several run-ins with raccoons–I decided the old "sleeping bag under the stars" wouldn't quite cut it anymore. I wanted something that made the great outdoors feel, well, a little less outdoorsy. Something warmer. Something raccoon-free. Something that flushed.

So several years ago, I made the command decision to buy a camper. Now we camp in heated luxury, with an RV just chock-full of extravagances like a roof, walls and all kinds of indoor plumbing.

Even with such opulence, the Princess and the Hobo have zero interest in camping nowadays, so it's just the Husband and me sitting in our fancy camper as he ogles the guy next door's breakfast meat.

"You better stop," I say. "He's going to see you, steaming up the window like that."

"I can't help it!" he exclaims. "It's bacon!"

I'm on my first cup of coffee, and it's way too early for this much excitement. "So?"

He sighs. "Why can't *we* have bacon?"

OK, now I'm pissed.

"Listen," I tell him. "I spent three-and-a-half hours packing this camper yesterday. There's chili, hot dogs, meatballs and lunch meat. I didn't want to deal with a bunch of bacon grease in a skillet I'd have to hand-wash. If you want bacon, pack your own damn bacon."

Ignoring me, the Husband sits up suddenly and leans closer to the window. "He went into his camper–but he left some bacon outside!"

"What are you going to do?" I ask. "Steal it?"

He considers. "Maybe!"

OK. He needs some pork-free distraction.

"You better step away from the window. Want to come sit with me at the table?"

He groans, rises from the couch and joins me at the little dinette booth, where he picks up a local map. I relax–I know he'll forget thievery for a while. After all, he loves maps almost as much as he loves bacon. This is a guy who will spend hours merrily paging through a Walmart atlas. I'm not kidding. I wish I was, but sadly, I'm not.

"I wonder where this road in front of the campground goes . . ." he says, tracing his finger along the line to the map's end on the table.

"Why don't you check it on your phone?" I ask.

He wrinkles his brow, annoyed. "Because I use *real* maps! I'm just a regular guy. I'm a 'Simple Man!'"

There he goes quoting Lynyrd Skynyrd again. Two can play that game.

"You got that right," I say. "Here. Give me your phone."

He hands over his iPhone, and I pull up the Google Maps app that I downloaded for him and he studiously ignores because he is, you guessed it, a Simple Man.

"See?" I say, pointing to our location on Google Maps. "You can trace that road to wherever it leads just by dragging your finger. It's downright magical!"

He scoffs, but takes his phone from me and begins poking at it. "My fingers are too fat. And what's this 'Explore Nearby' stuff?"

I snort. "I got something you can explore nearby . . ."

His head snaps up. I know how to get his attention—sex.

But like I said: first cup of coffee/too early for excitement. Luckily, I still know how to redirect his attention. How? You guessed it.

"I wonder if that guy ever took his bacon inside?" I ask.

He bounces out of the booth and plops back on the couch by the window. "It's still there!"

It occurs to me that I could continue toying with him in this manner, launching him between his favorite hobbies all day long, his head whipping back and forth Wimbledon-style.

"Look over there—possible bacon!"

"Come over here—potential sex!"

"Bacon!" "Sex!" "Bacon!" "Sex!" "Bacon!" "Sex!"—and of course the occasional "Maps!"

Oh, the fun I could have.

In a way, he deserves that kind of torture. Let's travel back through the years, before kids, before rustic/stupid camping, even, to our first wedding anniversary in 1996. We won't have to go far, because we spent our first anniversary here at this very campground in a "cabin." I put quotes around cabin for a reason. You see, it wasn't a "cabin."

It was a fucking Mouse House.

The Husband, ever the miser, had decided to spring $40 a night to rent a cabin at this campground as a first-anniversary surprise. I love the outdoors and getting away for the weekend, so I was pumped.

Until we arrived at said "cabin."

We pulled up to a small, dilapidated, lean-to type structure, outfitted with a dented front door and a single tiny window. I turned, wide-eyed, to look at him.

He shrugged. "Maybe it'll get better inside."

It did not get better inside.

We grabbed our bags, walked up the rotting front steps and opened the door to find an 8-by-8-foot room outfitted with folding chairs, a single light bulb and—wait for it—two kid-sized bunk beds. I repeat—bunk beds.

For the night of our first anniversary.

But the rotting wood, single bulb and bunk beds weren't even the worst of it. No sir. The worst of it was the mouse turds covering every single surface in the room. The floors, the chairs, the teeny-tiny bunk beds, all blanketed in little oblong pebbles of black mouse shit.

I'd have laughed if I wasn't already crying.

"Well, we won't be in here much anyway," said the Husband. "We'll be outside hiking and sitting by the fire!"

This, of course, is precisely when the rain started.

And the rain continued, pouring in buckets for hours. We sat in the folding chairs, twiddling our thumbs and staring at each other until we decided to brush the mouse turds off a small table and play cards.

Eventually, blessedly, hours passed and evening came. I grew hungry and begged for an escape.

"Please," I said, "get me out of here. Can we at least go up the road to Bob Evans or something?"

He tsked. "We brought a pack of hot dogs! What more do you want?"

At that, I gave up. Weak from misery, hunger and probably rodent-related Hantavirus, I crawled into one of the turd-covered single beds and spent the night of our first anniversary listening to the rain and the mice skittering across the floor.

They were hard to hear over my sobs.

Aw. Young love.

Here we sit, 25 years later in the same campground and a few hundred yards from the Mouse House of yore, which appears somewhat improved yet still entirely awful.

Let some other dummies endure it. I plan to stay in the camper, drink more coffee and look at my phone for a while until it's time to go outside, sit by the fire and drink wine for a while.

The Husband? It appears he plans to stare out the window and covet our neighbor's bacon.

But I'm not going to worry about it.

Because hey–I brought a pack of hot dogs.

What more does he want?

15
But Who's Counting?

You've been a loyal reader for several dozen pages now. So there's something important I really need to tell you:

I only have one year left.

Of work, that is. What did you think I meant? This is a humor book, people! You are here to laugh. I'm not going to write about my own death in a book about poor choices and large-breed dog poop. Sure, I'm racing toward the grave at a remarkable pace, and I'll tell you all about it soon enough. Probably multiple times. But I'm not going to speak of my demise. Yet.

I speak, of course, of retirement! That longed-for, lived-for time when the work is finally done and your life of leisure begins. Pitch the employee ID! Toss that nasty lunch bag! Throw your pants in the trash!

People, think of the freedom! The travel! The prospect of never wearing pants again!

OK, I'm using way too many exclamation points!

But that's just what happens when I think about retirement. I get all worked up and ready to take off my pants. Not for fun-zies, mind you, but for a nice, long nap.

My excitement for retirement began a few years ago when the Husband and I sat down one evening to discuss our future. I didn't really have high hopes for the conversation because I figured I'd be 100 years old before I could ever retire. Thanks to my questionable spending habits and decades of low-paying careers in creative fields (Never work in journalism or communications, kids!), when I pictured my golden years, I envisioned a hunchbacked old woman sipping cold soup in an unheated apartment and waiting to die.

Thankfully, the Husband had other ideas. Like I said last chapter, he is and always has been, shall we say, cheap, er, tight, I mean–frugal. He is even cheaper than I am. This is a man who checks his bank account balance three to four times a day. A guy who collects pens and pads from hotel rooms so we don't have to buy them. A dude who's driven without air conditioning for three boiling hot summers because "AC compressors cost too much!"

Knowing this, I shouldn't have been surprised when he informed me that thanks to his saving habits and overall tight-wadded-ness, we could retire in the fall of 2020–a date that was 78 months, or 6.5 years, away.

I jumped in his lap and hugged him. Seventy-eight months may still seem like a long time, but when you've been working since age 11, 78 months ain't so bad.

So I grabbed onto *78 months!* for all it was worth. I made a little sign for my cubicle that said *78 months!* and showed it to my co-workers. I then proceeded to annoy the shit out of them by announcing the updated countdown as I hung up a new little sign each month:

Seventy-seven months left! Forty-three months left! Thirty-nine months left!

They hate me now.

But I didn't mind, because the calendar kept flipping and the clock kept ticking down, down, down.

Now, here we are. One year. That's all. Twelve months. Three hundred sixty-five days. Eight thousand seven hundred sixty hours. Not that I am counting.

Friends have started asking, "What will you do with yourself?" To which I answer, "Nothing!" I want to do nothing. A whole lot of nothing. Great swaths of nothing.

I want to do nothing, but I wonder if I'll be able to do nothing. You see, I am bad at doing nothing. Terrible at doing nothing. Completely incapable of doing nothing.

The truth is that I've been trying to practice doing nothing for many years now, especially when I get home at the end of the week. First, I walk in the door and remove my pants. Second, because it is equally important as well as uncomfortable, I remove my bra. Next, I park myself on the couch and commence trying to do nothing.

Then, I start looking around the room. That's my first mistake. In every direction and on every surface, I see big obstacles to my goal of doing nothing: papers that need signed. Floors that need swept. Dogs that feel they need immediate attention.

So I close my eyes. Also a mistake, because there behind my eyelids lurk a thousand other chores and obligations. Meals to be cooked. Clothes to be washed. Overdue emails to be sent.

Closing the eyes doesn't work, so I open them again to find the rest of my family members, who are all excellent at doing nothing and already apparently retired.

The Hobo, for instance, lounges on the couch across the room mindlessly scrolling through Instagram. He's on a break from his oh-so-stressful schedule of playing video games and eating Doritos. Soon, he'll grab a Gatorade from the fridge and trudge back up the stairs to his room, where he'll stay until, oh, approximately 11 a.m. the following day.

The Princess, home from college, relaxes on the other end of the couch, also scrolling through Instagram. She's exhausted from watching me lug her dirty laundry downstairs so I can have the great honor of washing it. In an hour or so, she, too, will retire to bed, and won't make an appearance until late the next morning, when she smells the cinnamon rolls I've made for her.

The Husband has already retired to bed–his "office," he calls it–where he does almost everything, while simultaneously doing nothing at all. Eating, watching sports, checking the bank account multiple times a day, and yes, sleeping, he elevates nothingness/retirement to a high art form.

The dogs, well, they were born retired.

As they all lie sprawled hither and yon, I realize one thing: I'm flat-out jealous. I envy their inaction. Their lethargy. Their total and complete inertia.

Will I ever be able to do it? Nothing, that is? Will I ever be able to relax, let go, and just be a lazy retired turd like everyone else in my family?

I have a year left to keep practicing. Then, I imagine I'll spend the first six months pacing around the house, trying to force myself to do nothing. I'll have about as much success at this as I always do, so like every oldster before me, I'll end up volunteering somewhere for absolutely no salary whatsoever.

For now, I'll just enjoy the anticipation and the prospect of no more bosses, no more traffic, and definitely no more pants. I'll think about the glee, the delight, the absolute joy of the day in mid-September 2020 when I can leave my soulless cubicle behind.

And inevitably begin working again for free.

Oh well.

12 months left!

16
Life's Too Short to Live in Ohio

Spring, summer, fall and misery. Those are my four seasons.

I don't like the word "winter," because "winter" keeps trying to "kill me." Temperatures drop, the sun sets at, like, 3 p.m., and I become scared and confused. *Why are my lips blue?* I ask. *Why are my nostrils frozen shut? What happened to my will to live?*

After 50 years on this planet, you would think I'd get used to the concept of seasons and basic weather. But, no. Every year, I grow more shocked and appalled by the shit-show, the one that starts in November with plunging temperatures, strong winds and freezing rain. Next comes snow, which eventually thaws enough to cause an ankle-biting, bone-chilling crust. On top of this, guess what? More snow. Repeat this cycle for six months, or until you shoot yourself. Whichever comes first.

I'm thinking these happy thoughts on my way into work today. I have lots of time to think, creeping along as I am with hundreds of other drivers on an interstate coated in gleaming black ice. Overhead, flocks of geese fly south, calling, honking–laughing, it seems–at the predicament of the humans below.

"So long, morons!" they say. "Enjoy your morning commute!"

My hands are cramped into claws, gripping the wheel like a vise. But even so, I'm one of the lucky ones–dozens of cars have wrecked. Every few minutes, another dummy loses control and spins off the road. It's a metaphor, really: No matter how prepared you are and how carefully you proceed in life, sometimes it will toss you ass-over-tea kettle, right into the ditch.

And that's not the only lesson misery has taught me. Over the years, I have learned many valuable things, such as:

- The old college prank is true–you can indeed lift a Volkswagen Beetle. My neighbor Donny and I hoisted mine out of 3-foot-high snowdrift. My lower back will not forget it.
  Ever.
- During a power outage, home furnaces can be wired to gasoline-powered generators. In a pinch, this can be done by a chubby middle-aged mother of two, crouched amongst spiders using a cell phone screen as a flashlight.
- Shoveling the roof sounds stupid and dangerous. It is! To keep a structure standing under the weight of hundreds of pounds of snow and ice, it is also sometimes necessary.
- Icicles are lovely. Icicles can also back up inside gutters, thaw inside walls and cause leakage, mold and rot.
  Icicles are not lovely.

Now, true enough, I'm an Ohioan, and I should be used to misery. Ohioans don't expect rainbows and unicorns. We count on crappy weather. We thrive on crappy weather. We ARE crappy weather. Even in the best of months, our seasons suck. Fifty-five degrees one day, 5 inches of snow the next? Bring it on. Sunny warm breezes one hour, tornado warning the next? Sounds like the entire month of June. What else you got?

As a Buckeye, I pride myself on low standards, and each November, I pack up my flip-flops, my shorts and my smile. I don't bother looking out the windows anymore. There's nothing to see except gray and brown, so I close the blinds and try not to hang myself with the cords. Eating becomes a religion, cream cheese turns into a food group, and I settle in for six months of sadness, weight gain and Netflix.

Spring, summer, fall and Netflix. Also my four seasons.

Even though I've been in this state all my life, it wasn't my idea to stay. I'm stuck here because of the Husband's job. In the beginning of our marriage, I tried to get him to move. Lord knows, I tried.

"This is ridiculous," I said, blowing ice from my nasal passages. "Why can't we move to the beach?"

"Because I have a decent job, and I'll get a good pension someday," he said.

"But why can't you get another job down south? Don't they need cops everywhere?"

"Yes, but they don't always get a fair salary," he said. "Again, I say–decent job, good pension."

"Well, shit," I said.

We had this conversation in 1995. And in 2003. Also, last month. I keep asking, hoping the answer will change. But each time, it ends the same, with the *job*, the *pension*, the *someday* and the *shit*.

Part of the problem is–as someone who made the wise, wise decision to get a photojournalism degree–I do not know the thing called "pension." Writers and photographers have about as much job security as seasonal retail workers, and our employment in any given position has the lifespan of your average fruit fly. Most of us work many different places in our careers, never earning enough time in one spot to amount to a retirement savings. We're similarly challenged when it comes to salaries, just grateful to be paid anything at all to use our ever-so-valuable degrees in the creative field.

What can we say? Numbers are perplexing, man. Math hard. English easy.

There is good news, though, because thankfully, finally, someday is almost here. Yep, as I said last chapter, we're both retiring soon. Do you know what that means?

THIS IS MY LAST WINTER IN OHIO.

That's right. He's almost got his years in; I've cobbled together enough from my hundreds of jobs, and we'll soon be heading to the coast of Florida, where, as bonafide geezers, we're pretty much required to live by law.

I don't blame them. Have you seen that place? The sound of waves. The smell of flowers. The touch of soft sand. Each evening, heart-stopping sunsets with dolphins cresting in the distance and a rainbow opposite the setting sun. We go to Florida often, and each time, it's like a freakin' Disney movie. I'm pretty sure we found Nemo. The Husband has to bribe, coax and cajole me to come back.

"I don't worry about losing you to another man," he says. "I worry about losing you to another state."

Well, guess what, pal–you don't have to worry anymore, because you're coming with me. I'm already planning our escape, spending hours each morning combing Zillow for homes along the Gulf Coast.

Soon, very soon, we will get a little place. Then we shall pack up the kids, the idiot dogs, the formerly white couches, and like every good goose and geezer before us, we will–merrily, I say–get the fuck out of Dodge.

Just as God and the federal government intended.

So today as I sit on an icy black freeway with the dummies in the ditch, I know the end of misery is near. I have 273.93 days left of work–not that I'm counting. I smile and stare out the window at the v-shaped flocks of geese overhead, joyous, free, and laughing all the way out of town.

17
Who Are You People?

My family is being nice to me.

I am so very confused.

They're talking to me, listening to me and doing things with me. They're sitting with me, looking up from their phones when I speak, and sometimes, just sometimes, even laughing at my jokes.

What the hell? Who are these people?

They smile when I walk into the room. They respond when I ask them a question. They put their dishes in the dishwasher without "forgetting."

People, THEY HAVE BEEN CHANGING THE TOILET PAPER ROLL.

On Monday, the Hobo spoke to me as soon as he woke up. It was just a mumbled "Hi" in the hallway, but still. And later in the day when I asked him to go hiking with me, he said yes and didn't complain the entire time.

Then on Friday, oh wonderful Friday, the Princess came home from college and hugged me—*hugged me*, I tell you—spontaneously and of her own volition, with no one threatening her. Yes, you read it right, MY DAUGHTER HUGGED ME. This hasn't happened since the Bush administration.

Back in those days, neither one of them would leave me alone. That's how I was able to fill 181 pages of material for my first book, *I Love You. Now Go Away* with my family's constant desire to pester, harangue and otherwise annoy me.

But when the Hobo and the Princess became teens, our relationships completely changed. I went from being their favorite person—their mommy, their hero and the absolute love of their lives—to someone they just tolerate.

I know it's not me. After all, I still have the same parenting style. I'm still the same cool, awesome, really humble mom I've always been.

No, it's not me. It's them, and it's all completely normal for sweet, loving children to grow into morose, moody strangers who act like they can't stand their parents. Teenagers are horrible human beings. Everybody knows that. So this recent kindness they're exhibiting, though welcome, is most perplexing.

Honestly, it's not just the kids around here acting charming lately; the dogs, too, have been oddly well-behaved. For example, Suzie the Meth Lab, ever the spastic nitwit, has refrained from launching herself at visitors. Why it's been an entire three weeks since she has drawn blood from anyone at all. In addition, she's been staying away from the white couches, refraining from jumping on, rubbing against, or otherwise molesting them with her magnetic black fur.

Missy the Mastiff also has upped her "good dog" game. Normally, living with Missy is like living with a giant, devious coffee table whose goal is to sneak up behind and trip you as you turn around so that you drop whatever food you're carrying. Lately, however, she's become more aware of her formidable mass and hasn't been parking herself directly behind me. I haven't fallen over-top of her for two weeks, and she hasn't stepped on my feet for a month. My toenails are growing back. The scabs on my knees have healed. The doctor says I won't need surgery after all.

Not to be outdone by the dogs and the kids, even the Husband is on his best behavior. Just last Monday, he gave me a little rectangular box as I sat beside him on the couch.

"Here you go, Honey," he said, placing the black object in my lap.

I didn't know what it was. I hadn't seen one since my single years, so I eyed it suspiciously.

"What is that?"

"It's the remote control," he said.

"What's it for?" I asked.

"You know what it's for," he said. "You use it to change the TV channels and watch shows."

I couldn't believe my ears.

"Do you mean to tell me," I said, "that *I* am permitted to use the remote control? That *I* can use it to watch something *I* want to watch?"

He crossed his arms and glared at me. "Yes."

I picked up this "remote control" of which he spoke, held it toward my face, and turned it this way and that.

"Fascinating," I said. "I'm not quite sure what to do!"

He frowned and got up from the couch. "I was only trying to be nice."

I pushed the red buttons on the remote as he walked out of the room. *Holy crap*, I thought, *this is a brave new world.*

While flipping through the channels, dogs lying quietly at my feet, I pondered my family's newfound niceness. I hated to question this good fortune, but why in the world was everybody acting sweet to me? What the hell was going on? It felt weird—yet vaguely familiar—as if I'd dreamt about it in the past. The whole thing made me restless, so I kept pushing remote buttons, pondering my situation and trying to find something to watch.

After about 5 minutes of searching, I found it alright. Something to watch and something that solved the weird behavior of everyone around me. The show was *Rudolph the Red-Nosed Reindeer*. The answer to my family's weird recent kindness?

"A-HA!" I said out loud, to no one at all. "It's almost Christmas!"

Yep, thanks to Rudolph, I remembered that my family wasn't being nice to me. They were being *Christmas* Nice to me. How could I forget? I'd experienced Christmas Nice many, many times, and I could only blame my aging brain for forgetting that these days, my family is sweet to me for exactly two weeks in November, and three in December.

Because I do all the shopping.

And each year around this time, the family figures out that I'm the one with the debit card. I'm the one with the free time at work. I'm the one with the Amazon Prime account. I'm the one who makes the list, checks it twice and clicks "Add to Cart." I am Santa Claus.

That's right. Santa has boobs.

So you better be nice to her. After all, she knows if you've been bad or good, and you damn well better be good, for goodness sake.

You better talk to me, walk with me, smile at me and eat with me. You better hug me, sit beside me, hike with me and give the remote control to me. You better be kind, polite and very, very nice to me.

For about five weeks, anyway.

Inspired by my family's Christmas Nice, I wrote a song about Santa. And her boobs. Wanna hear it? All together now, to the tune of "Jingle Bell Rock."

Santa Claus, Santa Claus, Santa's a chick,
She lacks a dick, Santa's a chick,
No dude could do all they say that he does,
Only chicks could get all that done.

Santa Claus, Santa Claus, Santa's a chick
Ain't that a kick, Santa's a chick,
Bakin' and wrappin' and deckin' the hall,
With her wine bottle!

What a headache, how her back aches,

Fifty-nine things to do,
It's pure chaos, runs her ass off,
Most of these men don't even have a clue.

Santa Claus, Santa Claus, Santa's a girl,
All 'round the world, Santa's a girl,
Started her list around June 24,
Men they wait until the day before.

Santa Claus, Santa Claus, Santa has boobs,
Thirty-six Cs, average boobs,
Bouncing and flouncing all over the mall,
Since the early fall!

On Black Friday, she's up early,
Left before the crack of dawn,
Flat-screen TVs, she'd like one, please,
"I'm sorry ma'am—they're already gone."

Hurry up, Santa Chick, get the hell home,
Cookies don't make themselves,
Hubs he's asleep and he's no help at all,
That's why Santa's a . . .
Surely Santa's a . . .
That's why Santa's a chick!

18
Go Ahead–Throw the Book at Me

Over the years, I've made many, many, *many* poor choices. But the 80s were truly my Decade of Dumb.

Take 1987, for instance–senior year. Purple eyeliner, acid-washed jeans, unfortunate permed hair; boys, boys and still more boys. There are six poor choices right there.

I didn't think so then, though. Anyway, I was feeling really good because I'd just turned 18 and had recently purchased a vehicle so that I'd have a way to achieve my dream of attending ALL the parties.

It's good to have goals.

McDonald's job earnings paid for my ride, a 1984 Ford Ranger. But the McDonald's job also interfered with my mission of attending all the parties. So sometimes, I just didn't go to my McDonald's job.

Priorities. I had them.

It was during this Decade of Dumb that I had the pleasure of meeting the woman who would become one of my favorite teachers, mostly because she threw a book at my head.

We weren't exactly crazy about each other at first. She, for example, enjoyed telling me that she couldn't understand how someone with such horrible handwriting ended up in advanced placement English. She said I had the penmanship of a special-needs kindergartner.

"It really is amazing," she told me, many times. "You sure don't have the handwriting of a smart person."

But my writing wasn't the reason she threw a book at my head.

You gotta love the 80s, when a kid could be a kid and a teacher could throw stuff at a kid.

It's 2019 now, and these days, teachers would be fired and/or sued for such things. So even though she is probably long-retired and can't get in trouble anymore, I will call this teacher Miss Smith because I am original like that.

In fairness, she had every reason to throw things at me. I'd known about the 10-page term paper for nine weeks. It was a huge, multi-paged chunk of our passing grade, our ticket out of high school and into college.

And when did I choose to start this important work?

The day before.

It wasn't that I didn't want to write it. I just had more important things to do, such as attend parties and drive around town. Oh, and go to work at McDonald's—as long as there were no parties.

So it was that I found myself skipping school the morning before the paper's due date to stay home and get it done. Truancy, procrastination, sloppiness, all with a Guns 'n Roses soundtrack. That's how I rolled.

But I wasn't a very good felon, because when I sat down to scribble out my paper, I realized I'd forgotten all the needed books and notes in my locker, conveniently located directly outside Miss Smith's door.

Delinquency: not my strong suit.

Note to 80s self: Hi there, dummy. When skipping school to work on overdue homework, remember to take all the necessary books and papers with you the day before.

So, in the middle of "staying home sick" and frantically writing the term paper, I had to stop and drive my dumb ass to the school during the exact time of my AP English class. I parked, snuck in past Miss Smith's open classroom door to my locker, gathered the needed notes, attempted to quietly shut the locker door and …

CLANG!!!

Yeah. Locker doors aren't known for "quietly."

"I SEE you out there!" she yelled.

I cringed, then turned around. "Oh! Hi Miss Smith! How are you?"

My classmates snickered as she walked toward the hallway.

I proceeded to shit myself.

"How are *you*?" she said, glaring. "I thought you were home *sick* today?"

"Yeah, uh–but I forgot something and had to get it."

She narrowed her eyes. "Dawn," she said. "Do you have your term paper done?"

I swallowed hard, lowered my head, and feigned a deep interest in my shoes. "Yeah. Not just yet."

Her nostrils flared. "When did you *start* your term paper?"

My life as a felon was over. I would surely die now. "Um, today?"

Cue the crazy teacher eyes.

All 5 feet of her body tensed. She pivoted and balanced, flung her arm back, then pitched her heavy teacher's manual forward, directly at my thick skull and unfortunate hair.

Wow. She had a hell of an arm on her. I ducked just in time.

"Miss Smith?" I said, tiny-voiced. Even in my hunched-over state, I could see my classmates, 20-odd mouths wide open in shock.

"You've known about this the ENTIRE nine weeks! You just started today?"

She walked faster toward me, crazy teacher eyes blazing.

Well. Clearly, it was time for me to get back home to the business of truancy. Post-haste.

I ran out of school and drove home. Diet Cokes scattered around me, I plowed through an all-nighter and finished the paper, ending up in ample trouble with the principal for skipping school. I think I received a very generous, probably undeserved "C" for the piece.

Although I was in deep weeds with Miss Smith and the principal, there was one bit of good news: My mother had been at work the whole day and didn't know anything about my crime. So even though I received detention for skipping, I figured I'd still be able to keep driving around town after school, as well as attend ALL the parties.

I was wrong about that.

As it turned out, Miss Smith felt horrible about her actions. She called the house to apologize to my mother, who said, "I'm glad you threw a book at her. She deserved it," then hung up and grounded me for several weeks.

You may wonder why I say Miss Smith turned out to be one of my favorite teachers, when she yelled, threw things at my head and caused me to miss ALL the parties for weeks on end. There's a simple reason she's so special, and it is this: I never procrastinated again. Not once since my Decade of Dumb. Articles, scripts, essays, letters–my writing is *always* on-time, and sometimes even legible.

If it's typed.

To this very day, whenever I consider putting something off, I see flying books.

And crazy teacher eyes.

19
Excuses, Excuses

I hadn't even made it through the doorway before the Hobo bounded down the stairs.

"Hi, Mom!"

Startled, I almost dropped my purse. I never receive such an enthusiastic greeting from the boy these days—or any greeting at all for that matter. He's usually in his room or on the couch when I get home, buried eyeball deep in his phone or a video game. My presence generally elicits either no response or, at most, a half-hearted grunt.

"How was work?" he asked.

OK, something was definitely up. He'd done something bad. Or broke something. Or wrecked the car. So many horrifying possibilities. *Hmmm,* I thought, *Let's just see where this goes.*

"Hello, Hobo," I said, hanging up my purse. "Work was the same-old-same-old. How was school?"

"Good!" he said, trotting over to hug me.

Obviously, he'd killed someone. There was no other explanation for all this . . . interaction.

I pulled off my coat. "What is going on? What did you do?"

He leaned on the kitchen island, cupping his chin in his hands. "What do you mean?"

"I mean, why are you voluntarily talking to me and hugging me? You haven't done that in years."

He scoffed. "That's not true!"

"Yes, it is," I said. "You either did something or wrecked something or maybe killed someone, because otherwise, you'd be in your room or on your phone, ignoring me."

His mouth dropped open, feigning shock.

"So spill it," I continued. "What is up?"

"Well," he said, casting his eyes downward. "I was wondering..."

"A-ha! You *want* something."

He shuffled his feet. "I need a note for school tomorrow, so I can leave early."

"I see," I replied. "And why do you need to leave early?"

"Because it's December 20th."

"Um, December 20th is not a holiday," I said. "Your Christmas break starts next week, not this week."

"But it's almost the weekend!" he said.

This was getting fun. "So?"

"So nothing is going on," he said. "We're done with all our finals."

"I have to show up at work when nothing's going on and I'm done with all my stuff," I said. "It's called adulthood and it sucks."

"But, but," he stammered. "EVERYBODY ELSE IS DOING IT!"

And there it was, his final defense, his last hurrah. He'd thrown down the gauntlet, the old *Everybody else is doing it!* all wide-eyed and innocent, like it was a truth. Like I'd never heard it before. Ha ha ha!

Oh, son. I invented *Everybody else is doing it!* I invented wide-eyed and innocent.

At this point, I could've given in and written him a note, but I decided it would be much more fun to torture him for a while. In addition, all this unexpected conversation had caused at least a four-minute delay in my post-work ritual of taking off my pants as soon as I get home, which was making me cranky.

So I left him, agitated and confused, in the kitchen while I walked leisurely into the bedroom, removed my pants, shirt and bra and put on my pajamas at 6:30 p.m. the way God intended. Next, I used the bathroom, washed up, and leisurely brushed and flossed my teeth. Finally, I strolled–leisurely, mind you–back into the kitchen to find the Hobo. Still agitated, still confused, still right where I left him.

"Whatcha doin'?" I asked.

"I told you," he grumbled. "I need a note for tomorrow."

"And just what is this note supposed to say? You haven't given me any real reason why you shouldn't stay at school all day."

He threw his hands in the air. "Jeez! I don't know," he said. "I just know nothing is going on and everyone else is leaving, too. But fine. Whatever. I guess I'll stay all day. I'll be the only one there."

He stomped across the kitchen and back up the stairs.

Hee hee hee! I giggled to myself, happy I'd achieved my goal of teasing and annoying him. I didn't feel too bad about it, as he often derives a great deal of joy out of teasing and annoying me.

At least the Hobo had asked me for an excuse. Back in my Decade of Dumb, I was my mother whenever it suited me, happily signing her name to get out of school as often as possible. Indeed, I grew to be quite the expert at signing her name, which came in handy decades later when she developed dementia and couldn't write out checks for her bills anymore.

Who says crime doesn't pay? I'm here to tell you it *can* pay—all your confused old mom's overdue bills.

The point is that thanks to my formidable forgery skills, I took tardiness and truancy to a high art form in the 80s. I mean, I went to school late. I left school early. And sometimes, I just didn't go to school at all.

I wasn't my mother forever, though. There came a blissful day in 1987 when I didn't have to forge my way through high school anymore—the day I turned 18 and could legally write my own dang notes.

And oh, the many notes I wrote.

Several times a month, I wrote excuses for noon "dentist's appointments" so I could slip out to go to lunch with my other hooligan friends, some of whom had "dentist's appointments," too. Notes submitted, we fled the school building and drove to McDonald's, where we spent our parents' hard-earned money on greasy fast food.

Even though school rules prohibited leaving for lunch, we didn't feel the least bit guilty about our trips. No, we believed we were completely justified because our cafeteria served food they called "healthy" and "wholesome," but my friends and I felt it was more along the lines of "terrible" and "disgusting." So we fled the building, scarfed down McDonald's burgers and fries, and very much enjoyed our "dentist's appointments."

Still, we weren't complete delinquents; we didn't skip classes for the entire day. Fine upstanding students that we were, we always drove back to school after lunch for the rest of the afternoon.

Which turned out to be a mistake.

That's because our school principal had begun noticing a distinct upward trend of students disappearing at lunchtime. Because of this, he started staking out the parking lot. One fine day, after returning from a particularly satisfying "dentist appointment" wherein I'd enjoyed a juicy Quarter Pounder with cheese, I arrived back at school still shoving fries in my mouth just as he rounded the corner of the building. I parked, walked across the lot, and swiftly received a week-long series of detentions.

It was obvious I needed to rethink my system. Sitting in detention and pondering the situation, I decided that the notes weren't really what caused my apprehension. After all, the principal never said anything to me about the excuses; the problem was that I got caught coming back to school while eating french fries.

Clearly, the answer was to *not* come back to school.

Clearly, I was a genius.

The following Friday morning, I told my best friend, Amber, of my scheme. She agreed it was a great idea, so we devised a plan to leave at noon–and just not come back. That way, the principal could *not* catch us, and we would *not* get a detention, and, best of all, we'd foil his evil parking lot patrol.

We knew we wouldn't miss anything because it was a Friday and we'd already finished our school work for the week. So as soon as we got to homeroom that morning, we wrote notes for "doctor's appointments." We stayed a few hours, dropped the excuses off in the office at lunch time, and drove to my house, whereupon we spent the rest of the afternoon watching *Sixteen Candles*.

We did *not* go back to school. We did *not* get caught. We did *not* receive detention.

We did, however, split a warm six-pack of Old Milwaukee that we'd somehow procured, like a couple of middle-aged, unemployed alcoholics named Bill and Bob.

Do not judge us. School was boring and Bill and Bob were thirsty. Anyway, nothing was going on and everybody else was doing it, so why couldn't we?

Back home in the kitchen in 2019, I smiled as I recalled the day of Bill and Bob, always one of my favorite memories. But standing around and reminiscing wouldn't help me with the question of whether or not to give the Hobo an excuse.

Oh well, I thought, *he really is a good kid.* He also has nearly perfect attendance every year, as well as a 4.0 G.P.A. I decided to stop torturing him and just write the note.

Then I realized I had a problem.

Really, what the hell should I write? I mean, parents are supposed to be the proverbial adults in the room in matters of attendance; we're supposed to tell the truth on these things. And I'll admit I haven't always been 100 percent honest regarding the kids' excuses. I remembered a certain "outpatient surgery" note I wrote for the Princess that was actually for a trip to Disney World. *I am a horrible person*, I thought.

A horrible person who took her kids to Disney World.

I knew that for sanity's sake, it was OK to write the occasional excuse-fib. Otherwise, there would be no Disney trips, no afternoon movies, no Bill and Bob whatsoever.

Otherwise, there would be no fun.

And what would true excuses even look like? I tried to envision it for myself:

Please excuse me from coming to work today, as I don't have anything to wear.

Please excuse me from coming to work today, as I stayed up late last night to watch

Sixteen Candles. *Again.*

Please excuse me from coming into work today, as I just don't fucking feel like it.

Those are ridiculous excuses. Those are true excuses.

Those are AWESOME excuses.

But, in the Hobo's case, what to do, what to do? Should I lie, or should I truth?

Eventually, I decided that after so many years of lying, maybe it was time to change my ways. Especially because the current situation involved my son, someone for whom I'm supposed to set a good example.

And especially when the truth was much more fun.

I opened the junk drawer, pulled out a pen and a scrap of paper, and fulfilled the boy's wishes.

Please excuse Levi Weber on 12/20, as he says nothing is going on anyway, I wrote. *Plus, everybody else is doing it, so why can't he?*

Seems legit.

20
I'll Take the Shirt off Your Back

You may not know it from my current high-falutin', white couch-buyin' lifestyle, but I was once a poor kid.

Yeah, I know I said it earlier, but it bears repeating. So I'm putting it out there again in front of God, Google and everybody: My mother and I were broke as hell.

I'm talking poor, as in between paydays, we had boiled hot dogs for dinner. All week long.

I'm talking poor, as in when our tiny black-and-white TV broke, well, we just didn't have a TV.

For a year.

I'm talking poor as in Hills, Woolworth and Kmart discount stores for my blue jeans.

Let me repeat that so it sinks in: DISCOUNT STORES FOR MY BLUE JEANS.

The horror. The absolute horror.

I know, I know–kids all over the world were way worse off than I was. Some of them, I'm sure, had no clothes at all. But I was 15 and the center of my own universe, so one of my great and urgent concerns was that I didn't own a single pair of overpriced designer jeans. Hills, Woolworths, Kmart et. al. didn't sell designer jeans. They were only available at the mall, and my mother was emphatically *not* going to the mall.

"The mall is too damn expensive!" she said. "If you want fancy jeans, you'll have to get a job and buy them on your own."

Jeans weren't my worst problem, though. My worst problem?

Jim Bailey had my shirt.

Oh sure, he thought it was his shirt. After all, he was the one who had gone to the Cars concert and paid $10 for it. He was the one who'd been wearing it to school. Jim was a nice kid, a star basketball player and all-around decent guy, but still. He was not worthy of a shirt that should so rightfully be mine.

Because I was a Cars fan. A rabid, obsessed, maniacal Cars fan. I loved their quirky music and lead singer Ric Ocasek, who looked like a complete weirdo but still managed to be cool as hell. With acne and braces and Kmart clearance jeans, I, too, looked like a weirdo.

I, too, wished to be cool as hell.

The point is, I worshipped the Cars the way one should worship a god, and I didn't feel the least bit guilty about it. I'd gotten hooked on them after my friend Rick bought me a $4 counterfeit copy of "Heartbeat City" at the local street fair. Eventually, I obtained the rest of the catalogue thanks to another friend, Julie, who illegally dubbed all of her sister's Cars albums onto TDK cassettes for me.

What can I say? I had good friends.

Except for Jim Bailey.

He still had my shirt. True, he said he was my friend, but he wouldn't give me what was rightfully meant to be mine. I'd started asking him when he showed up at school in the shirt the day after the Cars concert.

"Hey Jim," I whispered to him in study hall. "You should totally give me that T-shirt!"

He looked up at me from his math book. "What?" he hissed. "No way."

"But I like the Cars way more than you do, so you should give it to me."

He returned to his book. "You're crazy."

Denied but unfazed, I tried again another day, right before Spanish class.

"Hey Jim," I said. "You're wearing my shirt."

He turned around in his seat and stared at me. "This is still *my* shirt."

"Yes," I replied. "But you should totally give it to me. I'm a bigger fan."

He shook his head and faced front. "You're crazy."

It went on for two years, the "Hey Jim/my shirt" and the "No way/you're crazy." Every time he wore it, we had the same conversation. And he didn't wear that shirt occasionally. He didn't wear it here and there. Nope. He wore it everywhere and every single week, torturing me and driving me to plot devious plans.

Maybe, I thought, I could trip him in the hallway and grab the shirt. Perhaps, I reasoned, I could tie him to a desk with my backpack strap, then pull it over his head. Or I could—and this was my favorite because of the potential for male nudity—sneak into the boys' locker room and snatch it.

I mean, the possibilities were endless.

Still, I knew forcibly stealing the shirt was a slippery slope. First you rip off someone's concert shirt, the next thing you know you're doing mob hits for Uncle Tony. And trust me—we lived just outside Youngstown.

We ALL had an Uncle Tony.

It was from the proverbial Uncle Tony that I found inspiration, as I watched Jim strut cheerfully down the hallway once again one day in what I knew in my heart to be my damn shirt. Two years had passed since he'd first worn it. Now I was 17 years old, wise, a bonafide woman of the world because I had something really big going for me.

A job.

That's right. Your little friend here was working at McDonald's, and yes, I flipped burgers. Hundreds and hundreds of burgers. Thousands and thousands of french fries. Billions and billions served. True, I called off a time or six so I could attend a party or six. But when I showed up, man, I worked. I mopped floors, scrubbed tables, cleaned restrooms, cooked McNuggets and served all manner of drunk, after-hours assholes. I did this and much more so I could finally buy a pair of fancy designer jeans.

In addition—and I'm not sure if I've mentioned it—but I had my eye on a shirt. A particular shirt.

And on that day in 1986, as Jim Bailey walked past wearing it yet again, I had cash from my latest McDonald's paycheck. *What would Uncle Tony do?* I thought, *if he had a little money in his pocket?* I realized that before he resorted to using force or committing outright theft, any proper Uncle Tony worth his weight in meatballs would first just try to buy the shirt for a good price. I didn't have to resort to violence after all. No sir.

Bribery. Extortion. This was the way to go.

I knew for a fact that Jim had only paid $10 for the Cars shirt, and because he'd been wearing it once a week for the past two years, the fabric had faded and the letters were peeling. Surely he wouldn't charge me very much. I'd just offer him small increments of money until he couldn't resist. My own little 80s Ebay.

So on that day in '86, I followed him to the cafeteria for lunch wearing my new designer jeans and glaring at his back all the way down the hall. *Gettin' real sick of your shit, Jim Bailey,* I thought.

He sat down at a table, and I plopped my backpack in front of him.

"Hello, Jim," I said. "I see you are once again wearing my shirt."

He bent over his lunch tray and started shoveling in food. "How many times do I have to tell you? It's *my* shirt, and I'm not giving it to you."

"Who said anything about giving it to me?" I sat and unzipped my backpack. "I am prepared to offer you up to FIVE DOLLARS for that old, faded shirt."

He laughed. "If it's so old and faded, why do you want it? Anyway, I paid $10."

"OK," I replaced the five and pulled out a $10 bill. "Ten dollars it is. Here you go."

The money on the table caught the attention of the other kids, who gathered around.

A gleam appeared in Jim's eye. "Hmm," he said, crossing his arms. "I'm not sure I want to sell it."

"I see," I pulled out the five again. "How about $15?"

He leaned back in his seat. "I mean, it *was* my first concert and all . . ."

I pulled out another five.

". . . and who knows when I'll get to go to another one . . ."

OK, obviously he saw an opportunity. Then again, so did I. Uncle Tony could play all day.

I put down another five.

"But I really don't want to sell it . . ."

And another.

". . . and my brother took me to the concert. He probably doesn't want me to sell it, either."

Repeat.

"Plus, it's just a cool shirt . . ."

I reached back into my backpack, felt around, hung my head and sighed. The other kids edged closer to the table.

It would be so easy, I thought, to just let my dream slip away at this point. I could keep my money, save it up, maybe even buy myself another pair of designer jeans. I could just give up and let Jim go on about his life peacefully, unmolested by my continual harassment.

But, really. What fun would that be?

I reached in a little further. Then slowly, slowly, ever so slowly, I lifted my head, smiled and slapped another $10 on the pile.

Forty-five American dollars now sat in front of Jim Bailey. Forty-five of my hard-earned, sweat-stained, greasy McDonald's dollars. "You should totally sell me that shirt," I said.

Eyes as wide as plates, he grabbed the money. "OK!" he said. "Alright already!"

"YEAHHHHHHH!!" the crowd around us erupted in cheers, high-fiving and bent over laughing.

I didn't know if they were cheering for me because I finally got what I wanted, or cheering for Jim because an idiot had just paid him $45 for a $10 T-shirt.

Probably the latter, but I didn't care. Like I said, the 80s were my Decade of Dumb. Anyway, the joke was on them: There had been a total of $60 in my backpack.

I'd have gladly spent it all.

Jim had to go to his locker and change, but sure enough he returned a few minutes later in his gym shirt, with the Cars T-shirt in his hands.

"You know," he said, "you are crazy."

I nodded, zipped my backpack, and stood up.
Then I grabbed *my* shirt, and I walked out of the cafeteria.
Like the motherfucking gangster I was.

21
He Drives Me Crazy

Farting, burping and professional testicle scratching.

These are the Husband's favorite hobbies, which I examined in great detail in my last book, *I Love You. Now Go Away: Confessions of a Woman with a Smartphone*. I recommend picking up several hundred copies so that you, your family and all your Facebook friends have an in-depth discussion guide.

Because this is an entirely different book, I'll let you know that farting, burping and ball-scratching aren't the Husband's only hobbies. There are many more, and new ones come along all the time. One of his latest hobbies is apparently driving through town like an old man. A very, very, VERY old man.

I shouldn't be surprised. He's recently developed several other elderly hobbies, including but not limited to obsessively reading the news, pulling his shorts up to his nipples and napping for hours on end–sometimes twice a day.

I get it, I do. We all become our parents; everyone knows that. Still, I didn't expect Mr. Weber to become, well, *Mister* Weber quite so soon.

Please, don't get me wrong–my father-in-law, the senior Mister Weber, is an amazing person. He's a good dad, a great provider and a former schoolteacher who also designed, built and ran two successful golf courses. He's now in his mid-80s, and he drives the way most people that age do: very, very slowly. There is absolutely nothing wrong with that. I hope I will do the same someday. Reflexes, eyesight and response times deteriorate as we age, and it's wise to take your time.

But the Husband is only in his early 50s and already driving this way. I noticed it a few minutes ago, as we crept down the driveway at the speed of snail, his foot on the brake and his head turning side to side as he surveyed the yard. All. The. Way. Down.

"Why in the world are you driving so slow down the driveway?" I asked.

He snorted. "At least I don't go like a bat out of hell, like you."

"But what are you staring at? You look in the woods then the yard, the woods then the yard, turning your head the whole time. All the way down!"

"I'm a police officer, okay?" he said. "There could be crime afoot."

"This town hasn't had a police report in 10 years," I said. "It's Brownsville. There is no crime because there's nothing to steal."

He ignored me and crept onto the side street in front of our house. At the rate he was going, it'd be another half hour before we made it the 200 feet to Route 40, so I settled in for the journey.

I thought his old-man driving hobby would be limited to the driveway and our little side streets. But I see he's also now driving like an 80-year-old in town, especially as we approach traffic signals.

For most people, green means go and red means stop. But as we head north on Ohio 79, I watch in alarm as the light ahead turns green, and instead of accelerating, he slows down and applies brakes. Side to side, side to side he turns his head, looking everywhere except through the windshield the same way he'd just done in the driveway.

Thinking this behavior is a fluke, I don't say anything at first. Until he slows down again at the next traffic light. And the next.

"You know . . ." I begin.

The Husband grows tense. *You know* . . . is my go-to signal that I'm about to offer him some Helpful Guidance™ on how he should do something.

"What?" he asks.

"Green means go, and red means stop."

"No shit."

It doesn't seem as though he catches my drift. I turn to face him, so he can better absorb my loving support. "Well, when the light is green, you're supposed to go through the intersection."

"Yeah. And?"

He still doesn't understand. Like an old man, he has no clue that he is driving like, well, an old man.

"When we approach the green lights, you've been putting on your brakes," I say. "You're slowing down instead of continuing on through. Plus, you keep looking out the side windows instead of through the windshield."

"Listen," he huffs. "I'm checking the intersections in case cross-traffic doesn't stop. I'm trying to avoid an accident. There could be crime afoot!"

"OK . . . " I nod. "But the people behind us have to slam on their brakes because you're unexpectedly applying yours when there is a green light. Which, you know, *could cause an accident.*"

"Hey," he says, *Hey* being his go-to *Shut the Fuck Up* signal that he's about to lose his temper with my Helpful Guidance™. "When I'm driving, I'll drive the way I want, and when you're driving, you drive the way you want."

"You never want me to drive," I say. "You don't like my driving."

He nods. "Exactly."

I turn back to face the windshield, resigned to my fate. I don't quite understand what's happening; he used to drive like a deranged lunatic–on the freeway, anyway. So much so that I dubbed him Swervy McDangerPants, and devoted an entire chapter in my last book–again, I recommend several hundred copies–to one of our terrifying, barf-inducing trips through Virginia. Perusing Mapquest maps at 80 miles per hour, 2 inches from the bumper of the car in front of him, side to side to side he swerved dangerously, as though the centerline of the road was just a suggestion.

"Why don't you pick a lane–any lane?" I asked him.

"Hey," he said, again with the *Shut the Fuck Up* shortcut. "There are 18 feet of roadway, I use all 18 feet."

But that was a long time ago. I have no idea if he still drives like a maniac on the freeway now that he's taken to oldster-driving everywhere else. I haven't been in the car with him in a while. You can see why.

I'll find out soon enough. After our errands here in Newark, we have to get on I-70 for a trip to Columbus. It's going to be quite a ride.

"You know . . . "

"Hey."

If the rest of today is any indication, we'll be creeping ever-so-slowly all the way to the city, his head turning side to side to side. In the end, I guess that'll be alright.

I mean after all–there could be crime afoot.

22
He Knows Not What He Speaks

The Husband knows lots of words. They're not real words; they're often the wrong words. But, still.

Words.

Most of his words aren't in the dictionary, or if they are, they're listed on another page with a different definition. You know, the correct one.

You may have guessed as much, but the Husband's name isn't really "the Husband," it's actually Joel. Thus, I've been calling his weird/incorrect words and phrases "Joelisms" because I, too, can make up words. I, too, can use them however the hell I want.

He and I have been together a long time, and he's always been afflicted with Joelisms. But in recent months they've become more frequent, incorrect and disturbing, as he descends into what is probably early-onset dementia.

Take, for example, a recent to-go dinner we'd ordered from a nice restaurant. We picked up our food, brought all the bags in from the car, unpacked the plastic carryout containers, sat down and began enjoying our meal.

I wasn't more than three bites in when I got hit broadside with a Joelism.

"Do you want, do you want your . . . " he asked, waving a small covered plastic ramekin in the air.

I looked up from my plate. "Huh?"

He wrinkled his brow and waved the ramekin around frantically, as though that would help him figure out words.

"You know," he said. "Your . . . your . . ."

I did know. But the situation was entertaining, so I felt it should continue.

"My what?"

"Your, your . . ." more waving, more bewilderment.

I tilted my head to the side. "Do I want what?"

"Your . . . your . . salad sauce!" he yelled, collapsing with relief.

This was going to be fun. I feigned ignorance.

"What do you mean, 'salad sauce'?"

"You know what I mean," he growled.

I took the ramekin from him and dumped the contents onto my salad. "Are you trying to say the phrase 'salad dressing'?"

"Nobody likes a smartass," he grumbled.

I smiled. "No," I said, "but I for one *do* enjoy a good *salad sauce.*"

He finished his meal in silence, while I tried not to laugh out loud. I'd like to say this was an isolated food-related Joelism, but it wasn't. A few weeks later, we were cleaning up dinner when he held up a fork.

"Did you use your spoon, or is it still clean?"

I was across the room loading the dishwasher, so I had to squint to see what he held, which was, again, a fork.

"What are you talking about?"

"Your spoon," he said, waving the fork.

"Well . . ." I said, as gently as I could, "that's a fork."

"You know what I mean!" he grumbled.

OK, now his affliction was starting to scare me. Maybe he should see a doctor; his spiraling dementia had begun escalating at an unbelievable pace.

To document his descent into Geezerville, I began keeping a list of Joelisms on my phone. I listed the Salad Sauce Incident, the Spoon/Fork Incident, his inventive mispronunciation of the word "botanical" as "Bott Annical," and last but not least, his whimsical description of a Swiss Army-type gadget I keep in my purse.

"Look at that," he exclaimed. "It also has a cork-the-screw!"

One of the best Joelisms occurred last weekend, as the Husband sat on the couch engaged in one of his favorite pastimes of watching movies he's already seen 100 times. The Hobo had just come down the stairs in search of his hourly snack, and he walked into the kitchen to search in what he calls the "Cupboard of the Junk Food (COJF)," a holy place of empty-calorie ecstasy.

The Husband snapped to attention as the boy opened its door.

"Hey," he said, "give me some of those . . . those strips."

The Hobo spun around from the COJF, perplexed. "Huh?"

"Those strips!" yelled the Husband, already annoyed.

"Dad," the boy reasoned, "what are you talking about?"

"Those . . . those . . . chewy meat strips!"

The Hobo, still confused, stood still. "Are you trying to say the words 'beef jerky'?"

"You know what I mean!"

The boy shook his head. "Not really," he said, grabbing a Little Debbie snack cake for himself and "chewy meat strips" for his father. He walked across the room. "See? This is called 'beef jerky.' Says right here, 'Great Value *Beef Jerky.*'"

The Husband grabbed the bag. "Nobody likes a smartass."

I picked up my phone to make note of the Great Chewy Meat Strips Incident of 2020. As I typed, it occurred to me that most Joelisms had been food- or drink-related, which is no coincidence. As he always says, "Men care about two things over the course of their lives: sex and food. I'm in the food phase."

So it wasn't surprising when he spewed yet another Joelism/food faux pas a few weeks later as we sat with friends discussing the possible origins of the COVID-19 pandemic in the wet markets of Wuhan, China. I'd just Googled a picture to show everyone images of the odd-looking mammals called pangolins, which are sold in wet markets and are rumored to be one of the virus's sources.

"Look at them," I said. "Aren't they odd?"

"Yeah," the Husband chimed in. "And they're consumed in China. They're considered a . . . a . . . delicatessen!"

I looked at him. And it would have been so easy. So obvious. So fun to correct him yet again.

Are you trying to say the word 'delicacy'?

I thought about pointing it out, but I didn't. Why embarrass him? I just thumbed over to the Notes app, typed "delicacy/delicatessen," and kept my mouth shut.

I knew what he meant. Plus, nobody likes a smartass.

Anyway, I prefer to mock him in private.

Or in a published, mass-produced book like this.

23
The Country Crock Chronicles

The Husband may be becoming his father, but there is no way I'll ever become my mother. Absolutely not.

That's because I am becoming my grandmother.

This I realized a few minutes ago after carefully rinsing, flattening and storing a used piece of plastic wrap. I'd shut the drawer and turned back to loading the dishwasher before it even hit me.

Holy crap, I thought. *Did I just rinse and save plastic wrap?*

I did. I did just rinse and save plastic wrap.

I reopened the drawer just to be certain. Sure enough, there it was–a damp piece of Saran Wrap, right next to a full box of brand new, never-used Saran Wrap. I'd cleaned and stored a small piece of plastic because I intended to use it again, just like my grandmother. I'd done this unconsciously, without even thinking about it, as if washing garbage is a perfectly normal practice.

I had to go sit down.

Head in my hands at the kitchen table, I'm now pondering my sad fate. How did it happen? How did I get so old, so weird? How did I become my grandmother?

In truth, there have been other signs over recent years. Consider that I, like her:

- Have never owned a couch without a slipcover. I don't like to even sit on an uncovered sofa, as I know that they're filthy and loaded with germs. True, my slipcovers are usually covered in dog hair. But at least they don't have hepatitis.
- My slipcovered couches are full of decorative pillows. Big pillows, small pillows, square pillows, circle pillows–if it's colorful,

uncomfortable and emblazoned with a cutesy saying, it's on my couch and directly in the way. If you don't like it, too bad. I'll be out shopping for more pillows.

- I go to bed early. Very early. Embarrassingly early. How early? So early I'm not even going to tell you. Suffice it to say that most people are cooking dinner when I go to sleep, and if it weren't for DVRs and on-demand, I would never see any prime-time television. Not only is the sun still out when I go to bed, it's high in the sky.

  The sun is my very own moon.

- The reason I go to bed so early is that I wake up so early. No matter how hard I try to sleep in, my eyes pop open way before the ass-crack of dawn—no pun on my name intended. I am up before my family. I am up before my friends. I am up before the neighbor's fucking annoying rooster. If it's dark, quiet and peaceful, my brain rouses itself and says, "Good morning! Time to worry, overthink and obsess about every stupid thing you've ever done!"

Even with all the above signs that I'm becoming my grandmother, the plastic wrap incident was a new low. I spent many hours in the 70s cheerfully mocking her for folding crumpled pieces of Saran Wrap to put in a drawer. You know, the way I'd just done.

"Grandma," I'd say, trying to contain myself, "Why are you reusing plastic wrap?"

She'd continue clearing the table, likely in search of more trash to wash. "That piece was clean. It was only covering a bowl of lettuce."

I'd open her junk drawer. "But you have a whole brand-new box."

"Well, there was nothing wrong with it. Why throw something away when you can reuse it?"

We had this conversation in 1975. Again in 1978. Also, 1979. No matter the year, it was always too much for me. I'd have to leave the kitchen to keep from laughing at her.

Ha ha ha! I thought. *I will never reuse plastic wrap.*

As time went on, I noticed Grandma's garbage fetish didn't stop at plastic wrap. Used aluminum foil also was carefully cleaned, folded, stored and reused, as was wax paper, along with old jelly jars she used for canning, egg cartons she used to start seedlings, and plastic milk jugs she used for . . . hell. I don't even know.

She built up quite the pile of all this stuff, so you'd think she would have eventually stopped. You'd think she'd have enough random trash. But nothing—I mean, nothing—could stop that woman from collecting . . .

. . . butter containers.

That's right, butter and margarine containers, and I mean all of them. Big ones, little ones, short ones, tall ones. The choices were endless really, because in the 70s, everyone ate butter, yet somehow no one was fat. So we all ate more butter.

My grandmother saw this as an opportunity and hoarded not only her containers but those from others at picnics, parties and potlucks. There wasn't a crappy plastic container in New Springfield–nay, all of northeast Ohio–safe from Laura's grasp.

She stored her collection on a special pantry shelf, meticulously organized with lids by size and butter/spread brand. Country Crock, Land O' Lakes, Shedd's Spread and more, all neatly stacked and–no lie–alphabetized.

Sometimes, I'd try to help her unload the dishwasher. But woe to the person caught touching her collectibles.

"No, no," she'd say, rushing over to grab a clean Parkay container from me. "I'll put it away. Stay away from my containers!"

I might have been young, but I was still big enough to know she had an issue. "Why do you keep so many butter dishes?"

"Because they're great for storage," she'd say, stacking the Parkay container in its Parkay spot with its Parkay brethren. "Plus, why throw something away when you can reuse it?"

"But you have enough containers for the whole town!" I'd say, mentally adding *because you* stole *containers from the whole town!*

At this point, she'd shrug and I'd just let it go because like her Saran Wrap fetish, her butter-dish thefts amused me. She wasn't doing any real harm hoarding them as they would have been tossed eventually anyway. I figured she was pretty innocent, all things considered.

Such was not the case with sweetener packets. Nope. When it came to sweetener, Grandma was a stone-cold thief.

At Denny's. At Eat n' Park. At the Ponderosa in Boardman, Ohio, my mother and I watched as my grandmother took every available Sweet'N Low packet, often before the waitress left the table.

We watched until we could watch no more, and one evening, we confronted her.

"Mother!" hissed my mom.

Grandma continued stuffing the packets in her purse. "What?"

Embarrassed, the waitress rushed away. "Why do you take those?" asked Mom.

"Because they're free."

"They're free for your drinks *in here*," I said. "Not for your drinks *at home.*"

"No, no," she said, waving us away. "They're free *for me.*"

For the rest of the meal, my mother and I avoided any eye contact with restaurant staff. The three of us finished and paid the bill at the cash register, and as we walked out the door, the waitress rushed over to refill the Sweet n' Low.

I still don't know why my grandmother thought she alone deserved free saccharine. Maybe she felt she was special. Maybe she figured she was old and could do whatever she wanted.

More than likely, she was supporting her addiction.

Because she had a vice. Not alcohol, not drugs–Granny wasn't a tweaker. Rather, she craved tea–really *sweet* tea. Sweet tea as in, "I'd like a little tea with my cancer-causing chemicals."

But Sweet'N Low was expensive at the time, at least for the wife of a retired salesman. Since my grandmother used six or more packets a day for her six or more cups of tea, she had quite the need to fill. Or the purse, as the case may be. So she'd steal more sweetener, stuff more purses, and sip more tea as my mother and I stared in disbelief, time after time after mortifying time.

Ha ha ha! I'd think. *I will never steal sweetener packets.*

That was more than 40 years ago, and I've kept that particular promise. I might save plastic wrap, but at least I don't steal Sweet'N Low, even though I use tons of it. I like a little coffee with my cancer-causing chemicals.

I also don't collect butter containers. Are you kidding me? I'm fat. I don't eat butter.

As if petty theft, tea addiction and butter-dish hoarding wasn't enough, Grandma had yet another issue:

She did not wear pants.

That sounds dirty, doesn't it? Like Gran was a perv or something. I don't mean it that way. What I mean is, well, indeed–Grandma didn't wear pants.

She wore dusters.

Dusters, otherwise known as housedresses, housecoats, or just plain ugly, are loose-fitting, casual dresses made of washable fabric, usually with snaps or zippers up the front. I didn't think you could buy them anymore, but you can; Amazon offers several with five-star reviews from ladies with names such as Betty, Martha and Mary Rose. Click out into the web, and a Google search of dusters will put you to sleep. So let me sum up the Wikipedia entry for you and say that dresses such as these are worn informally for household chores or quick errands.

That may be the case for some women, but when it came to my particular pants-less grandma, the "quick errands" thing absolutely did not apply. She would have died before letting anyone see her in her duster, which is how it came to pass that I bought all of Grandma's cigarettes.

Yes, this was a thing that actually happened. It was the 70s, OK? Kids weren't considered quite as "precious" as they are today. Lots of us worked as little servants and were expected to do many things for grownups. Things like mowing lawns, pumping gas, picking up mail, washing laundry, and buying smokes.

Or maybe it was just me.

Anywho.

My grandmother babysat me every day while my mother worked. About once a week, she'd notice her cigarette supply was running low and she needed more from the corner store.

Unfortunately, there was a problem: She wasn't wearing pants. She was wearing a duster.

She was *always* wearing a duster.

So she'd come out to the garage, where I was performing roller disco to a great big crowd of no one and grinding the cement floor to dust with my skates.

"I need you to go to the store for me," she said, squinting through clouds of pulverized concrete.

"Aw, Gran," I said, rolling my eyes and executing a perfect t-stop. I nodded toward the blaring AM radio. "They're playing really good songs right now. Didn't I just go for you? Are you out already?"

"Yes, I'm out. And you know Grandma can't go in her duster."

"Well . . ." I said. "Maybe you could put on pants?"

I figured I'd be wasting my time with such a suggestion, and I was correct. She shook her head and held out a piece of paper. "Here's your note. Be careful."

That is how one finds oneself, from age 9 and up, pedaling one's bike up the streets of New Springfield, Ohio to the corner store with a 5-dollar bill and a note that reads, "Please give Dawn one carton of Belair 100s. Thank you, Laura H."

Upon arriving at the store, I'd slap the money and note on the counter, and the cashier would give me the cigarettes without blinking an eye.

I went so often that eventually, I didn't even need the note anymore. Like I said: it was the 70s; things were different. Why not give the little girl a carton of cigarettes? Maybe throw in a fifth of vodka while you're at it.

I'd pedal back to my grandparents' house with one hand on the handlebars, one hand on the cigarettes, and absolutely no helmet on my head. Then, I'd carry the carton inside where I found good ol' Laura H. waiting for me anxiously and dusting concrete dust that had drifted in from the garage.

In her duster, of course.

"Here's your cigarettes," I'd grumble.

I always made it a point to express disgust, but honestly, I didn't mind the trips to the store. Cigarettes were awful, I knew. But I also knew they made her happy, and that's why I bought them for her.

Well, that and the fact that I had no choice.

As much as I disliked cigarettes, I really hated her dusters. To me, they signified everything wrong with the stereotypical idea of womanhood: garments designed strictly for cooking, cleaning, and child-rearing, to which my response was a resounding "Yuck."

But my grandmother spent her days–her entire life, really–doing these three things. Sometimes, she'd put on a nice dress and go out with my grandfather in the evening, but her daytime uniform was the duster. In it, she never left the house or, at most, the backyard. She was chained–by history, it seemed to me, or maybe her own low expectations–to life in a housedress. The work and the duster didn't seem to bother her too much. But in my eyes, they were oppressive, they were old-fashioned, and they were probably the reason she smoked.

They were everything I didn't want.

So I swore I'd never wear a duster as an adult. In fact, I vowed to avoid dresses altogether. My mother made me wear dresses for special occasions, and let me count the ways I hated them: the painful shoes, the tights and pantyhose, the never-ending crossing of the legs . . . Again, I said, "Yuck!" and you can guess what I said when I got older. That's right.

"Fuck!"

No way was I going to wear any dresses of any kind if I could help it. By God, I was going to put on some pants and conquer the world.

And that's what I did–minus the conquering the world part, of course. I pulled on pants and headed out the door and down the road to work like the rest of the dummies. For 35 years.

Over those years, the pants have grown ever tighter, more restricting and unpleasant. Pants are also inconvenient when a 50-year-old gal like me has to pee and I have to pee, well, anytime I'm awake.

As well as when I'm sleeping.

I know you're well-informed of my aversion to pants–it's been thoroughly documented in this book, my last book and likely will be explored in any future books. Sorry to repeat myself, but that is just how much I hate them. When I open the closet each weekday morning and pick out any pair of my ill-fitting, uncomfortable pants, I have a reaction that's visceral and altogether familiar.

It is, you guessed it: "Fuck!"

Thanks to said pants, it's true that I've been mostly successfully not wearing dresses for almost four decades. But while avoiding dusters and dresses, I've learned that pants sure aren't what I thought they were as a girl. See, pants don't mean "happiness." Pants don't mean "freedom." Pants don't mean "fulfillment."

Pants mean work.

Work: I am not a fan.

So these days, I remove my pants as soon as I get home from work and immediately put on pajamas, shorts, or my newest favorite, a beach dress.

What is a beach dress? Well, it's a loose-fitting, casual dress made of washable fabric that I wear at home.

I know, I know. Sounds familiar, doesn't it? But I buy these things on vacation, and they're printed with bright colors and flamingos and turtles and such. So they're beachy. So shut up.

The point is, they're comfortable and they're cute. Most of all, they're not pants, which is the entire point. You can call my dresses cover-ups, you can call them muumuus. But please, don't call them dusters.

Speaking of dusters, let me set aside my judgment for a minute, because I get it now, Gran. I get it. I love my muumuus, er, cover-ups, er, loose-fitting dresses. I mean, the comfort! The ease! The ability to pee at the drop of a panty!

And I know I made my grandmother sound like a duster-wearing, chain-smoking, butter-dish hoarding sweetener thief who sent her granddaughter–possibly illegally–to buy cigarettes. She was all those things. But she also was kind, generous and seemingly always in a good mood.

Probably because she never wore pants.

24
Spandex: Friend or Foe?

In a world where a reality star was elected president and leggings are considered pants, nothing should surprise me anymore.

Yet I'm surprised often. Usually by my own stupidity.

And while we're on the subject of legwear and surprises, I should point out that it is my pants and pants-purchasing habits that seem to inspire a good bit of stupidity, because I am incapable of buying pants that fit. Too big, too small, too tight, too loose–these eight words describe almost every pair of pants in my closet, and oh, there are a lot of pants in my closet.

I currently own 59 pairs of pants. Of these, approximately four pairs fit. Yet I keep buying them. Work pants, sweat pants, yoga pants, jeans, slacks and chinos, they're all heaped on a shelf in my closet that sags under the weight of too many pants. The shelf has no more room, so I gave up and started piling them on the floor like a homeless drug addict.

Like I said, if it were up to me, I wouldn't even wear pants. I'd much rather walk around in a beach dress, my comfy underwear, or better yet, nothing at all. Unfortunately, I'm required by law, the workplace and my children to cover myself. Pesky societal norms.

I could wear other garments on my lower half, but I choose pants over skirts and dresses because put quite simply, I am too old and fat to cross my legs all day. Crossing your legs when you're old and fat is like attempting to stretch two rubber bands–two painful, taut, fat rubber bands–from your very sore hip sockets to your very sore knees. If you do manage to get your legs crossed, you'll soon go numb because once you reach a certain age, blood circulation sucks. Upon getting up and trying to walk, you'll stumble around on pins and needles groaning and complaining like the gross fat geezer you are.

Yes, folks, the future is bright.

Because I am one of the above gross fat geezers, I buy lots of pants. And because I am a knucklehead, I don't buy pants in my size.

Instead, I buy pants that are too small. I'll see a pair of pants on the clearance rack and think, *These are super cute! Plus, they're on sale!*

Unfortunately, most clearance pants are tiny. But that never stops me. No sir. Why?

Because I'm going to lose a bunch of weight!

Someday!

I purchase the too-small pants and take them home, waiting for someday when I lose a bunch of weight.

Someday–shocker!–never comes, and the too-small pants bind, pinch, pull and give me wedgies. To compensate, I go out and buy pants that are way too big.

It is a vicious, expensive, ridiculous cycle.

I am the queen of ill-fitting pants.

I keep the pants, big and small, in the closet and on my crackhead floor pile. I look at them, ogle them and sometimes try them on. *This pair is too small,* I think. *This pair is too big.* None of them are just right.

Despite my 59 pairs of pants, the one type of legwear I'd always avoided was leggings, the uber-tight stretchy pieces of spandex that grew popular on university campuses and spread like an unsightly plague across the entire country. Why did I avoid them?

BECAUSE LEGGINGS ARE NOT PANTS!

You can tell by the shouty capitals that I FEEL STRONGLY ABOUT THIS.

That's because in my day, we called tiny stretchy bottoms like these "tights," and they belonged *under* clothing–usually skirts or very long sweaters–as an extra layer to keep the legs warm

Told you I was old.

About five or six years ago, some college coed somewhere rolled out of bed, looked at a pair of tights and said, "I'm wearing these and nothing else!" then pulled them on.

Now, I will admit that leggings look ok–albeit a bit slutty–on little college asses. That's how they get away with wearing what amounts to nothing.

Unfortunately, older women soon decided they too could wear leggings and display their large, lumbering rear ends for all the world to see. Kudos to them, I guess, for not caring. Yet every time I encountered a woman over 35 flouncing around in $80 LuLaroe, I had the urge to shout, "LEGGINGS ARE NOT PANTS!" and punch her in the throat.

I knew for sure that I'd never wear them. See info re: gross fat geezer above. In addition, my ass and thighs seem to be the final resting place of every potato chip that's ever crossed my lips. Ruffles have ridges, y'all. Nobody wanna see that.

So, no. I didn't think I'd be wearing leggings anytime soon. I hadn't even touched a pair first-hand until the Princess came home from Ohio State one weekend and I had the distinct honor of washing Her Highness's laundry.

While pulling clean clothes from the dryer, I found a pair of what appeared to be–gah!–leggings. Her leggings.

I started to fold them, but then stopped because they were just so . . . soft. And warm. It was winter, I was freezing down there in the basement, and I felt very tempted to try them. Just to see how they felt, you know, just for giggles.

I didn't think it would be doable. She has a little college ass, and as I said, I possess a Ruffles ass.

Still, she and I are of a similar height and build, so even though I weighed about 25 pounds more, I held up the leggings, stretched the spandex a couple feet wide and figured maybe it could happen. Stranger things have occurred in this world–see sentence re: reality star/president above.

I peeked up the stairs to make sure she wasn't coming. Then, I sat down on the basement floor and began pulling them on.

I tugged.

I yanked.

I jerked and I sweated.

But guess what? I got them up eventually. And guess what else? They were soft. They were warm.

They were really, REALLY comfortable.

No binding, no pinching, no pulling and no wedgies. Just comfort. I could even cross my legs. Briefly, but still–it felt like I was wearing nothing. Probably because I was pretty much wearing nothing.

Then again, wearing nothing has always been a goal of mine.

Thus began my leggings era. I purchased a few pairs of my own, which were much easier to put on once I found some in my size. They are warm, soft and REALLY comfortable, and of my 59 pairs of pants, leggings feel like the only ones that genuinely fit. So wear them I do.

But only at home.

Why?

BECAUSE LEGGINGS ARE STILL NOT PANTS!

And like I told you: Ruffles have ridges, y'all.

Nobody wanna see that.

25
Pull up a Couch

Work from home? I'll do you one better than that. Work from couch.

That's where I am. It's mid-March, 2020, and the world is in the midst of the COVID-19 pandemic. Face masks. Empty shelves. Packed hospitals. Roads? Deserted. Parking lots? Empty. Few people go out of their houses, and most of those who do wear masks and rubber gloves. The whole thing is pretty much the beginning of every apocalypse show ever. The first episode of *The Walking Dead* featured this exact plot, and we all know how that turned out.

But far be it from me to bring everyone down. The news isn't all bad. I'm here to tell you there's a bright side to the impending doom, and it is this:

No pants. Absolutely none whatsoever. And no bra, either–if you're a woman.

Or just a dude who digs lingerie.

Thanks to COVID-19, most people are working from home just like me. In fact, we were told to work from home. *Due to the COVID-19 outbreak, we ask that employees telecommute for the foreseeable future* was the email we received. It should have said, *Due to the COVID-19 outbreak, we ask that employees telecommute and remain pants-free for the foreseeable future.*

I only speak from experience. Today, I drove to work on a deserted interstate only to be instructed to go back to my house and work. I was floored. Although most companies allow employees to occasionally telecommute, it never happens for me because I'm employed by the state. This is similar to serving in the military, only stricter. The general public and people who have private-sector jobs think state employees have it made, and maybe 50 years ago, they did. These days, however, staties receive only average benefits and lower salaries than their private-sector counterparts, and we are expected to always report to our offices, even in Level 3 snow emergencies.

So for the State of Ohio to permit employees to work from home was shocking to say the least. It took a literal apocalypse to make it happen.

They didn't have to tell me twice. My boss excused me at 9:44 a.m. I left at 9:45 a.m. I arrived back at the house at 10:45 a.m. and removed my pants and bra at 10:46 a.m. I put on my PJs at 10:47 a.m.

Then, I gathered my laptop and walked out to the living room.

"Aren't you supposed to take your pajamas off this time of day, instead of putting them on?" asked the Hobo, already in quarantine and in my spot on the chaise/couch.

"They said I had to work from home," I said. "They didn't say I had to wear pants to work from home."

He continued scrolling his phone, still oblivious to the fact that he was in my God-given seat.

"Yo, you're on my chaise. That's where I'm going to work."

"Can't you 'work' over there?" he asked, nodding toward the other dog-hair covered couch.

"No," I said, "but you can go scroll Twitter over there."

He rose from the seat, but not before scoffing, tsk-ing, sighing and doling out all the other expressions of teenage annoyance that I've learned to ignore. He thumped up the stairs to his room, leaving me to answer email exactly the way nature intended: on the couch, without pants or a bra.

Now this, I thought, *this is the way to work.*

I've long suspected that I could happily telecommute thanks to some very deep thoughts I've had over the past 15 years in my workplace cubicle, such as:

- I am uncomfortable because . . .
- I'm forced to wear pants, and . . .
- a bra, also. . .
- my chair sucks . . .
- because it isn't a couch.

In addition, I've always known that I could do about 99 percent of my job at home. I mean, what do I do each day? I check email and write scripts and articles that are assigned to me via said email. How do I do this? With Microsoft Word. On a laptop. Of which I have two at home. With Microsoft Word.

All located conveniently near my couch.

It's probably the same for you. What do you do all day? Probably check email, and complete projects assigned to you via said email with programs available to you on laptops. Of which you likely have several, all located conveniently near your couch.

And guess what? If we all worked from home, we'd be much happier. I found the following very scientific information on the internet, therefore it must be true. Studies have shown that working from couch, er, home:

- Boosts productivity
- Increases employee satisfaction
- Reduces costs for office space, utilities and supplies
- Allows employers to hire the best talent, anywhere in the world
- Increases employee loyalty
- Results in fewer sick days

With benefits like these, it's just ridiculous to travel to an office when we have all the available technology to telework. Also, do the math: Five of the seven days in a week, we spend half or more of our waking hours at jobs. HALF! We give more hours to our employers than we do our own families. We're spending too much time away from our homes. We're spending too much time away from our children.

We are spending too much time away from our COUCHES.

So, people of America, I beseech you: Just do it. Settle in, hunker down, and get to work on your own dog-hair covered couch. Launch your email, pop open a Word doc, and nestle under your softest blanket, completely pants- and bra-free.

It's true, this pandemic could do us all in. But what a way to go.

26
TP Apocalypse

I could wipe with that.

Such are the obsessions one has during the time of plague. I do, anyway. Not hand-washing, not mask-wearing, no. My thoughts turn repeatedly and compulsively to . . .

. . . wiping. Not my nose.

My butt.

Apologies for the graphic visual. But it's the third week of the coronavirus pandemic and I'm a little worried. Aside from working from couch without pants or a bra, about the only good things to come of COVID-19 is that A) I'm still here–so far, and B) I can now reliably spell the word "apocalypse." So needless to say, I'm a little edgy.

Things are so weird and awful right now that state governments have issued stay-at-home orders and shut down schools, restaurants and worst of all, bars. Stores have cut their hours, limited the number of shoppers inside and completely sold out of toilet paper.

Ugh. No bars and no toilet paper. Whatever will we do? However will we WIPE?

When I'm brave enough to don a mask and gloves and go to the store, I see the TP shortage firsthand. Shelves–hell, entire toilet paper aisles–are completely bare of Charmin, Cottonelle, even that terrible White Cloud. The entire paper goods aisle is empty and taped with caution tape, exactly like a murder scene. You can see straight through the shelving to the snacks aisle and onward, into the very bowels of hell.

Toilet paper isn't the only thing missing; meat is hard to find, and vegetables have completely disappeared. Normally you can't give veggies away, but finding a bag of romaine lettuce right now is impossible. It's like the world is ending and everybody decided to sit down for a nice Caesar salad.

Still, it's the lack of TP that keeps me up at night, and for that, I blame the Husband. When the COVID-19 epidemic started a month or so ago, I foresaw the impending Shortage of Doom and asked him to pick up three extra packages of toilet paper for us on his weekly Sunday grocery trip. Did he do that?

Of course he didn't. Spending money on something we already have at home causes his tightwad head to explode. He bought exactly one pack of toilet paper. And guess what? As of last Wednesday, we didn't have much left.

The thing is, I don't even like toilet paper. Honestly, I hate it. I prefer bidets, and we will get to that soon enough. The reason I am no fan of toilet paper is that like so many women who've had babies, my undercarriage has been through the wringer. The Hobo's birth was especially traumatic on account of his giant head, causing one maternity nurse to tell me that in 30 years of medicine, she'd never seen a bottom as terrorized as mine. "It's like a bomb went off down there!" she said.

I will try to spare you the rest of the gory details, but suffice it to say my southern hemisphere has seen it all: constipation, hemorrhoids–all the things women complain about after having a baby. In my case, the baby is now 17, and I'm still a mess–such was (and still is) the size of his head. Sometimes it's so painful I don't know what the hell is going on back there. It's like an army of knife-wielding elves, cheerfully taking turns stabbing me. When you're that sore even the softest Charmin feels like 60-grit.

What can I say, though? A girl's gotta clean herself, and as the old song goes, you don't know what you got till it's gone. Or almost gone, anyway, and since this TP shortage started a few weeks ago, I've been looking at toilet paper as gold. Better than gold, actually. I'd happily trade one of my good necklaces for a value pack of Cottonelle.

I've been forced to plan ahead. To really look around. For things with which to potentially wipe. Nothing has been safe from my gaze. And really, the possibilities are endless if you're imaginative. Leaves? I could wipe with that. Old napkins from the glove compartment? I could wipe with that. Ears of corn? I could wipe with that. The dogs? Don't tempt me, because if I have to, I will absolutely wipe with them.

In the very beginning of the pandemic, my saving grace was the local Dollar General. Surrounded by cornfields and cows, it sits alone with no other nearby businesses. The parking lot is always packed, though, precisely because there's nothing else around and we don't have a choice. It's about a mile down the road from our house in Beautiful Downtown Brownsville near another small village called Gratiot, which we pronounce improperly as "Gray-shot" because we are rednecks. We love our Dollar General because it sells all kinds of necessities. Cigarettes, Mountain Dew, plastic wading pools. Really, what more does a hillbilly need?

Since regular big-box grocery stores became coronavirus-infested cesspools devoid of veggies, meat and toilet paper, I'd been staying away from them as much as possible and hitting up the Dollar General whenever we needed something. But eventually, DG didn't have TP either, so I gave up and went back to thinking creatively. We never completely ran out of toilet paper, but I was planning ahead in case we did. An old towel? I could wipe with that. A Post-It note? I could wipe with that. One of the Husband's clean socks? I could wipe with that, then maybe put it back in his drawer. It would certainly serve him right for not buying extra toilet paper when I told him to.

Thinking of things with which to wipe has become my favorite hobby, and I was deep in *I could wipe with that* mode while driving back from the Gratiot (Gray-shot) post office the day before yesterday. Because of their disappointing lack of wiping items, I'd recently started ignoring good ol' DG. They'd disappointed me. They'd let me down. They'd completely run out of toilet paper.

I was just getting ready to turn and drive past the store again when a little voice whispered to me. *Never doubt the Dollar General*, it said, so I turned my head and surveyed the store's parking lot.

And what to my wondering eyes did appear? A great big semi, pulled up to the cement pad of the side dock. *Hmm*, I thought. Semis meant boxes. Boxes meant items. Items meant stocked shelves.

I pulled into the lot and parked. I grabbed my purse, jumped out and almost ran to the paper goods aisle where I found . . .

. . . absolutely nothing at all. Of course not. Why did I even bother?

Head down, I turned and began walking back toward the doors when I saw something out of the corner of my eye.

One employee, dressed in yellow and black. Opening a great big box of motherfuckin' toilet paper.

My heart leaped. I snuck up on her slowly, carefully, the way one would approach a rabbit. I didn't want to spook her, lest she dash away with the loot. I waited until she disappeared behind a shelf. Then, I made my move, lunging at the box and thrusting my arms inside.

Which is, of course, precisely when she came back around the corner. There I was, caught. Guilty. Red-handed.

Arms full of packages, I tried to plead my case.

"Please, miss," I said. "May I have some?"

She hesitated. "Yeah, I guess. But you can only take two. If you absolutely need them."

"Oh I do, I do! Thank you so much!" I reduced my armload to two packages before she changed her mind, avoiding the urge to hug her.

I turned around and nearly skipped to the register, where I smiled triumphantly at everyone around me. A woman behind me whispered, "Where did you get it?"

"It's in the back," I hissed. "Not on the shelves, still in the box. The other employee is unpacking it. She'll let you have two!"

She spun on her heel and sprinted away, intent on her own mission.

Still smiling like a fool, I paid for my purchase, walked out the door and drove home with my "DG" brand TP.

DG was the cheapo store brand. It would feel like steel wool, I knew. I didn't care. As I said, my rear is a war zone anyway. At least I had something with which to wipe it.

And so with this, my lowly TP adventure, I hope I have helped you during your time of need. Remember, if you're ever running low on toilet paper, just get creative, stay alert and take a page from my book.

Because you know—you could totally wipe with that.

27
Butt-Washin' Bliss

Ah . . . nothing I love more than a good gadget. If it's expensive, unnecessary and *As Seen on TV!* I probably own it.

Or at least have it in my Amazon shopping cart.

Unfortunately, my affinity for such items has caused me to make a lot of very bad gadget-related decisions. The heated eyelash curler that didn't curl. The Magic Strain colander that didn't strain. The Miracle Thaw meat thawer that thawed nothing but my cold, dead heart. The list goes on and on, and they were all bad decisions. I've spent hundreds of dollars on miracle this and magic that, only to end up disappointed and broke.

But if you've been paying attention, you'll notice that I don't let common sense stop me. No sir. I believe in *Magic!* I believe in *Miracles!*

I believe in *As Seen on TV!*

Because sometimes–just sometimes–these gizmos work. And even though this is a book about bad ideas and poor decisions, I'm here to tell you that last week, I made a fantastic gadget purchase. It was a *Miracle!* It was *Magic!*

It was a *bidet!*

Go ahead–laugh it up. Everyone else does, and the Husband sure did. He teased me. He badgered me. Oh, how he mocked me.

We first encountered a bidet in 2005 while staying in a fancy resort room in Mexico. Located in the bathroom, the bidet was dark blue porcelain and looked a lot like the nearby toilet, with the exception of a dial near the back instead of a flush handle.

Initially, I was skeeved out by the bidet. I knew it was for butt-washing, but where exactly did the water come from? I guessed–wrongly, I might add–that the water floated up from the bowl itself for the butt-washing experience. Surely the pot was a seething soup of viruses, germs and bacteria from the many fat American asses it had hosted. No bueno.

But (butt) upon further examination, I saw the bidet had a nozzle apparatus connected to the freshwater supply at the wall. This allowed only clean water to spray upon the rear, thereby rinsing it and directing any, um, dirt down into the bowl, and then into the drain. The setup reminded me of sitz bath apparatuses women use after childbirth, designed to cleanse and comfort our very sore, very violated undercarriages. I remembered how clean I felt after those baths, and how nice it felt not to drag toilet paper through the raw, violent minefield that was my postpartum rear end.

So after a thorough inspection, I decided to give the bidet a try. What did I have to lose? After all, Mexico is famous for its water. What could possibly go wrong?

In addition, I knew that tourists visited Cancun to live dangerously, experience new things, and possibly get murdered by the cartel. *I'm probably going to die here anyway*, I thought. *Might as well go out fresh.*

To avoid the Husband's interruption, commentary and judgment, I locked the bathroom door. Then, I sat. I squirted.

And lo, I was clean.

My first bidet experience was, to say the least, life-changing. The ease! The comfort! The unparalleled cleanliness! It was just like a sitz bath, without all that pesky childbirth.

I walked out of that Mexican bathroom a new woman. A changed woman.

A woman who wanted a bidet.

"Guess what?" I asked the Husband, who sat in an easy chair across the room engaged in his favorite vacation hobby of reading travel brochures.

"What?"

"I just tried the bidet!"

He looked up at me, nearly dropping his pamphlets. "Why in the world would you do that? Is there no toilet paper?"

"Yeah, there's toilet paper," I said. "But I wanted to try the bidet."

He snorted. "What are you? Some kind of . . . European?" His belly shook with laughter. "No, wait. Yer-a-poopin,' so you used the bidet. Ha ha ha!"

That's how the mockery began. Every time I stepped back into our hotel room from the bathroom, he stood there, waiting and smirking.

"How was your buddy, the bidet?"

"Am I being replaced?"

"Do you need a cigarette?"

I tried to tell him I used the bidet solely for purity. It was, for me, anyway, like a car wash, a veritable power-washer level of pressure, and not to be toyed with. The bidet was strictly for business–not pleasure.

Of course, he wasn't having any of that, and he razzed me all through the Cancun trip, all the way home and onward, ad infinitum.

So for years, I tried to forget my little Mexican friend. But I couldn't do it, because Holy Hygiene, Mary—the purity! The ease of use!

The bidet! It called to me.

Unfortunately, our bathroom is much too small for such a big, bulky item. Like I said, bidets are the size of toilets, and our washroom barely fits the toilet we have let alone an additional one. I thought about buying another sitz bath to achieve my hygienic goals, but I remembered the bath's cumbersome bowl and the long hose that attached to the bathroom sink. Way too much work. I decided to give up my dreams and continue using toilet paper.

And I got along ok, I guess.

OK, that is, until last week.

When we started to run out toilet paper because of the coronavirus pandemic and I couldn't find any suitable thing with which to wipe, I panicked. When I panic, I Google.

When I Google, I gadget.

That's when I found it. My hope, my dream, my holy grail. A $60 gizmo called the *Luxe Bidet Toilet Attachment*. I literally ran for my debit card. Quick—add to cart! Take my money! Two-day shipping! By Friday at 1:15, I'd received my package. By 1:30, I'd installed it.

Then, the angels sang.

The *Luxe Bidet Toilet Attachment* connected to our existing toilet. The water came from the supply line underneath the current commode, then the nozzle and dial apparatus attached to the toilet seat. It was easy to install, even easier to use. And people, put your judgment aside for a minute because let me tell you—this thing works.

I cannot describe the happiness I felt as I used my *Luxe Bidet Toilet Attachment* for the first time. It was like Cancun, 2005 all over again, but with less cartel. Once again, I knew the unfettered joy of a squeaky clean ass. Plus, I didn't have to worry about running out of toilet paper anymore. No paper products? No problem! Ha! I laugh at your TP apocalypse.

Friday evening, the Husband saw me smiling as I left the bathroom and knew something was going on. As a person who's fought constipation since the Clinton administration, the words "smiling" and "bathroom" don't usually go together for me.

"What's up with you?" he asked. "Why are you so happy?"

"I bought a bidet attachment for the toilet. It works so well!"

"Great," he said, rolling his eyes. "Another gadget. We're in the middle of a pandemic and a collapsing economy, and you're buying butt-washers."

"Well, thanks to the fact that you didn't get extra toilet paper when I asked you to, we are going to run out. When that happens, you'll be able to use the bidet."

"No way am I using it," he said. "I don't need that thing."

"You shouldn't say that to someone who sees and washes your underwear," I said.

He ignored me and walked away, shaking his head. "You and your bidets," he said. "You and your gadgets."

That was only the beginning of a new chapter of harassment from him. He teased me, he badgered me, oh, how he mocked me—yet again. Then he told the Hobo and our friends, who did the same.

You know what, though? I don't care at all. They can say what they want because I believe in *Magic!* I believe in *Miracles!* I believe in *bidets!*

And I am clean as a whistle. Let the gross wipers of the world keep using their nasty toilet paper. They probably won't be able to find it in the stores right now, but if they do, let them wipe and wipe and wipe. Let them drag the proverbial peanut butter through the proverbial shag carpeting.

Just like a bunch of savages.

28
Illegal in Several States

It happens to almost everyone eventually. You're going along living your life, dreaming your dreams and merrily walking around without ever having a tube inserted in your personal regions, when all of a sudden . . .

BAM!

It's time for your first colonoscopy.

Yes, despite your best efforts to avoid such a situation, chances are you will one day find your butt staring down the business end of a colonoscope–a very long tube with a camera. Now, "butt" and "very long tube" are not words anyone wants to see in the same sentence because, when placed together, they sound like bad ideas. Horrible ideas.

Extremely painful ideas.

Yet, either due to your age or the fact that you're having GI problems, you're bound to butt-face a colonoscopy one day. So here at the Center for Helpful Guidance™, we've put together a handy guide for women in this very situation, as I, um, have a woman "friend" who recently experienced it. Please, read on:

- Suffer painful pooper problems for several weeks. Dread telling any doctors about it, because you think it will lead to medical staff poking around in your coal hole, and of course you are eventually right about this. Be sure to begin worrying incessantly and imagining the worst.
- Google your symptoms on WebMD, otherwise known as It'sProbablyFatal.com. Obtain lots of information, all of which basically boils down to "Could be nothing. Could be cancer." Proceed to have nervous breakdown.
- A month later at your annual OB/GYN appointment, discuss

symptoms with physician. Although he used to briefly examine your rear prison purse in addition to your front lady garden, he tells you insurance companies no longer allow him to enter the back door unless there is bleeding. "It's probably nothing. You'll be fine," he says, recommending fiber and water, both of which you already consume, and sending you on your way.

- Two months later, head to family doctor and tell her about ongoing problems. "It's probably nothing. You'll be fine," she says, also prescribing fiber and water, which again, you already consume. She doesn't examine your poop pocket, either. You're finding out that oddly, no one wants to look inside your butt, even if you pay them.

- Symptoms continue for several more months, so you make an appointment with a specialist, who is concerned enough to prescribe a colonoscopy. You are very relieved that someone will finally be looking inside your butt. You are extremely horrified that someone will finally be looking inside your butt.
And snaking a hose all the way up your Hershey Highway.

- As colonoscopy approaches, begin dreaming of snakes–in doctor's offices, in toilets, in your underpants. For good measure, make repeated visits to WebMD/It'sProbablyFatal.com and continue to scare yourself silly. Chant *It's probably nothing. You'll be fine!* every night until you fall asleep.

- On day before procedure, limit diet to such satisfying items as water, tea and lemonade. Obtain can of chicken broth. This is your lunch. Later that afternoon, open giant prescription bottle of MoviPrep, a.k.a. Colon Blow. This is your dinner.

- Gather fully charged iPad, ten-pack of toilet paper and a change of underwear. Sprint to bathroom and strap yourself to toilet, for it will be your new home. Over the next eight hours, you will excrete digested food from as far back as the Carter administration exiting your rear at speeds approaching the sound barrier. At times you think you will be done with your terrifying mission. But you will be wrong.

- Around midnight, attempt to sleep. Note the word "attempt" here, because thanks to the fact that you can't eat, drink, or take any of your usual fun array of sleeping pills, you will be wide awake, starving and riddled with anxiety. Your husband's snoring keeps you up, so you head to the couch, where your growling stomach keeps you up. Seriously contemplate eating throw pillows.

- Arrive at hospital the next morning and check in. Thanks to worry and eight hours of tossing and turning, you're half asleep yet still

conscious enough to be scared, well, shit-less. (See what we did there?)
- Allow medical staff to prep you for procedure, and smile weakly at their attempts to cheer you up with poo-related humor. You're desperately trying to forget the fact that they'll soon be doing things to you that are illegal in several states, so you ask for anesthesia. The nurse obliges, but you feel nothing at first and tell her, "I don't think you gave me enough. I'm really nervous so you'll probably need to inject more 'cause I don't feel a thing and . . . zzzz."
- Wake up groggy and half-naked with faces all around you, as if you've slept through your first orgy. The doctor says everything looks fine, and you're suddenly very happy because of this great news, not to mention the awesome anesthesia. Despite your liaison with the pooper python, you feel no pain in your rear end. In fact, you feel no pain at all.
- Head into recovery area. A nurse checks your vitals and says that you have to pass a large amount of gas before she can release you. You cheerfully oblige her request in front of God and everybody, because you know this is the quickest route to food. Also you are still high as a kite.
- Giggle while husband helps you dress and ties your shoes. As you haven't eaten since dinnertime two days ago, demand that he takes you to Taco Bell, like, "At once!" and "Post-haste!"
- He reminds you that you've recently consumed 64 ounces of MoviPrep/Colon Blow. *Hmm,* you think, *Taco Bell, Colon Blow* . . . Even in your purple haze, you realize that combination is a bad idea. So you ask him to take you instead to Bob Evans, where you consume everything on the breakfast menu. And the contents of the butter dish.
With a spoon.

Well, there you have it, folks, a handy Helpful Guidance™ guide for your first trip down the old dirt road. You can see that a colonoscopy is a horrifying way to take awesome drugs and freak way the hell out about nothing, as well as a chance to get naked, sleep and fart.

In front of total strangers.

29
No Clothes? No Problem!

I was so excited that I forgot my pants.

Yep. Sure did. In my haste to get the hell out of Ohio, I left the house for a week's vacation without packing any pants whatsoever.

True, my trip was to Sarasota. But still. It was going to be *January* in Sarasota. Mid-winter temps can sink as low as 50 degrees, especially at night, and if it's me who's in Florida, you can plan on that being the high for the day. To an Ohioan in January, 50 degrees isn't bad, however, 50 does necessitate pants. Which as I said, I'd completely forgotten.

I know what you're thinking: *Were you even wearing pants when you left?*

A valid question.

And yes, I was wearing pants in the form of jeans for my flight. But one pair of jeans for an entire week of vacation does not a wardrobe make. I'd packed six pairs of shorts, underwear, and T-shirts and, in a fit of optimism, I packed two swimsuits. To add insult to injury, the jeans I wore for my flight weren't even 100 percent clean, as I'd chosen a pair I'd already worn once due to the Fat Girl Stretch Factor.

What is the Fat Girl Stretch Factor, you ask? Well, for a lady of leisurely proportions like myself, putting on freshly washed jeans from the dryer is not fun. It's a struggle that requires stamina, sweat and Herculean effort, much like a snake swallowing a giant bullfrog, the snake being the jeans and the giant bullfrog being me.

In the Fat Girl Stretch Factor, the giant bullfrog/fatty wears the jeans a time or two to stretch them out, thereby conquering the snake/jeans by providing maximum expansion in the belly and buttocks region. This gives a chubby gal room to move, breathe and/or sit on an airplane for several hours. Bullfrog: breathing. Snake: conquered.

Back to my original story of forgetting pants. So there I was, driving to the airport at zero-dark-thirty in my day-old jeans and realizing that in my haste to flee Ohio, I'd forgotten to bring any suitable clothing for January in Florida. Despite this bonehead move, I wasn't too worried. *You're an Ohioan,* I thought. *Fifty degrees is downright balmy.*

And that's when my phone rang.

"Hello?"

"Hi," said the Husband. He was a few miles behind me on the interstate, driving to work.

"Yes . . ." I said, curious as to why he'd called. After all, I'd just told him goodbye not 25 minutes before.

"I was just wondering," he said. "Did you take your suitcase?"

Oh HELL no.

I dropped the phone and waved my right hand frantically across the backseat, where I found four umbrellas, eight reusable shopping bags, and absolutely zero suitcases.

"Shit!" I said, grabbing my phone back from the console. "You're right–I didn't bring it. I packed it but I forgot to put it into the car!"

"I thought so," he said. "I remembered it was sitting in the kitchen. But then I didn't remember you taking it out the door. You better turn around."

"Shit!" I repeated, hanging up on him and searching for the nearest exit.

Forgetting pants was the least of my problems—because I'd forgotten my ENTIRE SUITCASE.

I had retrieved the suitcase from the basement, packed it full of skimpy summer clothes and no pants, and put it in the kitchen where it now sat, uselessly surrounded by dog hair. Then I walked right out the door without it.

Already halfway to the airport, I exited I-70 at Ohio 310, drove over the interstate and got right back on again like the nitwit I am. I hurried home, grabbed the suitcase, startled the dogs and jumped in the car. Again.

Racing back to the airport, I wondered how in the world someone could do something so asinine. How could one plan for a trip, pack for a trip and begin actually *going on the trip* without luggage? I mean, it was somewhat understandable that I'd forgotten my pants, because I hate them. So yes, forgetting pants was, in my case, plausible. But worse than that, I'd forgotten my shirts, pajamas, bras, underwear and toothbrush, and walked out of the house as if I owned nothing, just like a bum. Fa la la.

Stupid. Dumb, dumb and dumber. How did I get so dumb?

In truth, this incident was only one of several I'd had in recent weeks. Perhaps the dumbest thing I'd done was wash my hair.

Bear with me here.

For several days leading up to my trip, I'd been washing my hair–as one does. The problem was you couldn't tell I'd been washing my hair, as every single day it got more greasy and filthy-looking.

Figuring I wasn't washing it enough, I dumped tons of shampoo in my hand and scrubbed harder. I used my fingertips and nails and really got in there, scraping my scalp as hard as I could to remove the dirt and grease. That didn't work, either.

So I bought a gadget called a shampoo brush. I dumped the shampoo on it and rubbed it in with the brush, scrub-scrub-scrubbing tracks in my head with the hard rubber nubs. But still–no luck. My hair remained gross as hell.

Soon enough, I gave up. I figured maybe the greasiness was some kind of horrible-yet-unsurprising middle-aged phenomenon I didn't know about yet. Just another 50-year-old fun fact. *I guess this is just who I am now*, I thought. *Greasy and fat and 50.*

It took a while to solve the mystery. A few days later, I reached into my shower caddy and pulled out the dirty washcloths to launder them. As I lifted the last one, it knocked over my shampoo bottle.

Only it wasn't my shampoo bottle. It was my conditioner bottle.

I'd been shampooing, scraping and scrubbing my hair *with conditioner*. The reason my hair had been so greasy in recent days was that I'd been washing it with basically more grease.

A.k.a. conditioner.

I rushed into airport parking thinking about the recent conditioner debacle. *Maybe this is all related*, I thought. *Maybe I forgot my pants and my suitcase because all that conditioner/grease seeped into my brain and clogged it up, making it even foggier than before.*

But I had no more time to waste thinking about it. I parked, jumped out, grabbed my things and made it to the gate for the flight to Sarasota with barely a minute to spare.

Seated on the plane, my heart still pounding, I leaned back and tried to relax. But I couldn't help worrying that I'd continue my streak of stupid on the trip by mixing up the shampoo and conditioner again.

I shouldn't have worried. When I stepped into the shower the first time, I realized that would never happen.

Because I forgot to pack it.

30
Hotel Hepatitis

Eating Doritos. Killing my plants. Competitive farting.

Those are the three main activities of the Husband and the Hobo when I'm gone, judging by the empty bags, acrid air and bone-dry rosemary plant on the windowsill. The Princess is off at college, and I've just walked in the door from another solo trip to the beach, during which I slept, sunbathed and enjoyed a box of wine without judgment, commentary or interruption. It was beautiful, relaxing and entirely fart-free.

Being away from my family doesn't happen often. When it does, both sides secretly enjoy the break. I look forward to the time alone—to think, to read, to slowly savor a nice box of wine.

The boys look forward to a frat party. They buy Doritos. They buy sugary drinks. They consume said Doritos and drinks in questionable clothing, crumbs falling carefree to the floor. For them, life is good because I'm not around advising them on all the things they should and shouldn't do.

And I can see it's time to dole out some direction now that I'm back home. Observe, if you will, the living room, where the Husband sits on a couch covered in crumbs and dog hair. There are snacks. There are drinks. He is happy.

Now, let's climb up the stairs to the Hobo's room, where he's permanently hunched over his computer because I haven't been around to offer my input on his shitty posture. There are snacks. There are drinks. He is happy.

It's a mess here. But despite the crumbs, mess, farting, dead plants and general lack of good posture, it is great to be back in Beautiful Downtown Brownsville with these barbarians. As lovely as my solo vacation was, the trip home must have been some kind of karmic payback.

See, to save money and appease the ever miserly Husband, I drove south this time instead of flying. This meant a 16-hour drive split between two days, and a night spent in a motel.

A cheap motel.

An awful motel.

Oh, that motel. I'd booked it on Expedia, seduced by the low, low price of $44 a night. I should have known better, but in my defense, the pictures of the place looked fine–nice, even. In addition, it wasn't like it was a Motel 6 or something. It was a "Travelodge by Wyndham." I'd normally avoid the "Travelodge" part, but Wyndhams are usually decent, so I rolled the dice.

And boy, did I lose.

Upon pulling into the lot, I noticed that the hotel looked nothing like the pictures on the website–they'd apparently used stock corporate photos of another building. In addition, even though the "Travelodge by Wyndham" was advertised as a hotel, it was definitely a *motel*, with no interior corridors and cars parked just outside the exterior rooms. It had a look that screamed bedbugs. It had a look that screamed sex.

It had a look that screamed hepatitis.

Obviously, it had been a stupid decision to book a place based on price and the word "Wyndham." But I'd been on the road for 12 hours. I was exhausted, cranky and I just wanted to go to bed, so I crossed my fingers and pulled into a parking spot. I checked in with a pleasant-enough attendant and got back in the car to drive around to my room.

Well, I thought. *She seemed nice. Plus, it's a Wyndham. It can't be all that bad!*

But, whoa. Was I wrong.

I opened the door, and almost turned and ran. In fact, I absolutely should have turned around and run for the nearest Hampton Inn, miserly husband be damned.

I didn't, though. I was mesmerized by the horror of what I saw, not registering that I'd actually have to stay in what was a complete train wreck–if the train had been full of porn stars. Filthy carpeting. Stained walls. Furniture that appeared to have been purchased at a police auction.

From a crime.

That happened in 1974.

As I stepped through the doorway, I could hear various creatures scurry away, running for their lives. I began searching for a place to put down my bag, one without dirt or dried DNA. Wooden table? Crusty food. Dresser? Sticky surface. Floor? Might as well dip the bag in the toilet, then roll it in a bucket of bedbugs.

Finally, I settled on a metal shelf bolted high on the bathroom wall.

Oh, the bathroom.

I've never seen another hotel/motel bathroom like it, and I hope to never see one again. It was a handicapped bathroom, which wouldn't have been a problem except it appeared to be a handicapped bathroom for Larry Flynt, complete with filthy, suspicious tile and a giant walk-in shower large enough for Larry and four of his *Hustler* girls. And–the um, icing on the cake, so to speak–an archaic, rusty beer bottle opener screwed into the front of the bathroom sink.

I repeat: a rusty bottle opener *on the front of the bathroom sink.*

Don't get me wrong. I am a huge fan of beer bottle openers and own several myself. I, too, enjoy convenience.

I, too, prefer beer that's open.

It's just that I've never seen a beer bottle opener attached to the front of a hotel/motel sink, patiently waiting for the next drunken fool to arrive at 2 a.m. If the bottle opener had been new, clean, or located near the ice bucket in the room, it would have made sense. But this opener–ancient, filthy and oxidized–was bolted proudly on the sink, directly next to the toilet. It was a look that said, "Sit down, crack a brew, take a dump. I'm here to serve you."

Once my eyes stopped burning at the sight of Larry Flynt's shitter, I turned back to the rest of the room and stared in terror at the bed with its flat pillows, thin mattress and dark brown frame, all of which appeared to have come directly from the set of *The Rockford Files*. And then, the bedspread.

Cue horror music

Again, we call to mind the work of Larry Flynt: disco colors, garish patterns, and stiff. Very stiff.

So, so stiff.

I nearly cried. But again, I'd been driving 12 hours. I was beyond tired, and somewhere between the Larry Flynt bottle opener and the Larry Flynt bedspread, I just gave up.

There was one stroke of luck in the whole terrifying situation: I'd brought a blanket in my car. It wasn't much, but I figured if I covered myself with it, I'd at least have some protection from the seething, pathogen-coated sheets.

Grabbing a "clean" towel from the bathroom, I lifted the bedspread and blanket from the bed and tossed it onto the floor. I then retrieved my blanket from the car, wrapped myself head to toe, and launched backward onto the mattress.

I said a silent prayer, and slept the sleep of the damned.

The next morning I awoke at dawn, jumped out of bed and directly into my shoes. I grabbed my bag and blanket and left without showering or using the toilet, so as to avoid the Larry Flynt situation as much as possible. I hopped into my clean, STD-free car, happy to be alive.

Four hours later, I'm here at the house. I can see that for the entire week

I was gone, the table hasn't been wiped, the plants haven't been watered and absolutely no vegetables were consumed. I wonder if they even bathed. It's like *Animal House* up in here. It's gross. It smells. It's a complete and utter dumpster fire.

It is not, however, the "Travelodge by Wyndham" in Wytheville, Virginia.

It is home.

We have pathogens, sure, but they are *our* pathogens. Like I always say, there are no germs like home germs.

After doling out some Helpful Guidance™ to the Husband and the Hobo, I take my bags and blanket to the basement, dump it all into the washer and set the dial to "sanitize."

I climb back up the stairs, step over the mastiff and the Meth Lab, and throw myself beside the Husband on the couch, where he sits, dazed and drooling into the Doritos.

31
Jeff Probst: He Haunts Me

It's not every day you see a hot celebrity walking down the street in Ohio. But I saw one yesterday.

In my dreams, of course.

There he was: Jeff Probst, the host of *Survivor*. Just strolling on the sidewalk like it was nothin'. Ooh-la-la.

I know what you're thinking: *Why is she talking about hot celebrities? Isn't she married?* The answer is yes, and happily so. I am married, but I'm also not dead, and the truth is most married folks will admit to a celebrity crush, a.k.a. "free pass," which is a famous person that, hypothetically, a spouse will let you, um, "dally with" if given the chance. Of course, you will never get that chance, especially in Ohio.

Still, it is nice to dream.

The Husband's free pass/celebrity crush is Sandra Bullock. The way his eyes light up when they come on-screen, I also suspect he's got an imaginary free pass for both Jennifer Aniston and Angelina Jolie as if he were an imaginary Brad Pitt. I have several free passes, including Bruce Springsteen, who is way too old for me, Anderson Cooper, who would never be interested, and my dear, dirty Mike Rowe.

Mmmm... Mike Rowe. I've got a dirty job for you, Mike Rowe.

All of the above guys are great-looking, talented and funny, and none of them sport a beard or mustache–two things I dislike. Most importantly, they all seem to be extremely nice, good-hearted men. I have a theory borne from my years of dating that most extremely handsome men are neither nice nor good-hearted. They don't have to be–everything is handed to them. So they tend to be easy on the eyes and hard on the heart, and I learned early on to avoid them as much as possible. My particular husband is the exception to the rule, as he's both handsome and good-hearted. So I snapped him up as soon as I could. He didn't stand a chance.

But enough about him. Back to other nice, handsome men. Far and away my favorite celebrity crush, my hottest free pass, my boo, is *Survivor* host Jeff Probst. I have unclean thoughts about him almost daily, so it would have been nice to do unclean things with him in my dream.

I am, after all, only human. And have you seen this guy? Twinkling eyes, great hair, fit body, and dimples . . . oh! Those dimples. It's like all the Greek gods joined forces and conjured up the most perfect male specimen the world has ever seen for the sole purpose of hosting a reality show. In fact, *Survivor* is television's longest-running reality show, and there are two reasons for that: Jeff Probst's right dimple, and Jeff Probst's left dimple.

Being a fan of both dimples, I watched most of the *Survivor*'s 40 seasons on Amazon Prime and ponied up $10 a month for the rest on CBS All Access so I could devour each and every episode. As I watched, I noted that not only is Probst physically perfect, he's funny, easy-going, extremely nice, and often serves as a makeshift therapist for *Survivor's* contestants.

Lucky them. I'd lie on his couch any day.

Finishing all 40 seasons/540 episodes of *Survivor* must have caused my Jeff Probst dream, which began in Beautiful Downtown Brownsville. I was walking down the sidewalk admiring the cows, cornfields and double-wide trailers when up ahead I saw someone approaching in the opposite direction. As the figure drew nearer, I couldn't believe my eyes.

That hair. That body. And oh! Those dimples.

I stopped in my tracks, searching for the right words to say—words that could hopefully lead to unclean acts with none other than Jeff Probst.

I needed something hot. Something sexy. Something he couldn't resist.

What did I say, you ask?

"Jeff Probst! What's up?"

That's right. Even in my dreams, the very best I could come up with upon seeing the man who, husband aside, ranks as the hottest man on earth to me was "What's up?"

And what did Jeff Probst do after hearing my sexy, sexy words? He smiled. He waved. He smiled and waved.

Oh! Those dimples.

Still, the smile and wave were the extent of my imaginary sexual encounter with Jeff Probst. I guess that's how it is when you're a 50-year-old woman with the sex drive of a chair. An old, tired, lumpy chair.

Unmoved by my super-hot greeting, Jeff kept walking down the street, so I went back home to a toddler-aged Princess and Hobo, and colored with them at the kitchen table. This was wonderful until we spilled an entire box of crayons—I'm talking Crayola 64-pack (with Built-in Sharpener!)—all over the floor and had to pick them up, one by one by freaking one.

Picking up a Crayola 64-pack will give you a lot of time to think, and so I thought of—you guessed it—Jeff Probst, and my brilliant pickup line, "What's up?"

Even in my dream, I knew lame-o greetings like that are the story of my life. I can write clever, coherent sentences to express myself all day long, but there is some kind of disconnect between my brain and my mouth that trips me up when I talk to others. It's especially true in stressful situations like conflicts or celebrity sightings, when I have a tendency to choke up or spew inane idiocy. You'll agree with me if we ever meet. I am very disappointing in person.

Oh well, I thought, *Jeff Probst would never go for an old, tired, lumpy chair like me.*

That's when I heard it.

Tap-tap-tap-tap-tap.

What was that? More importantly, *who* was that? Someone knocking on the window? On the door? I waited.

Tap-tap-tap-tap-tap.

There it was again! Could it be my free pass, my boo? Could it be Jeff Probst, knocking on the door in my dream?

Tap-tap-tap-tap-tap.

I threw down the crayons, ran to the door, opened it . . .

. . . and promptly woke up, to . . .

. . . *tap-tap-tap-tap-tap.*

The Husband's razor.

Tap-tap-tap-tap-tap.

Hitting the side of the sink.

I rolled out of bed and walked to the bathroom, where the Husband—and sadly, not Jeff Probst—stood *tap-tap-tapping* over the damn sink.

"Thanks a lot," I said. "You woke me up with all that noise."

"It's Monday," he said. "I have a bunch of whiskers to shave from the weekend."

I sat down on the toilet. "Can't you just skip it sometimes? You're so . . . LOUD."

Tap-tap-tap-tap-tap. "You know I have to shave for work. And I thought that you didn't like facial hair?"

No, I thought, *but I like Jeff Probst an awful fucking lot.*

Finished on the toilet, I pulled up my pants and nudged him out of the way so I could wash my hands. The soap mixed with his shaving cream and little black hairs, all of it swirling down the drain.

I turned to leave the bathroom, whereupon the Husband used his free hand to smack my ass, which he does daily, hourly and any time he's near me. I swung my hand back and slapped his arm, which I do any time he does that.

I looked at the clock: 5:40 a.m. I knew I'd never get back to sleep with all the racket. Plus, by now, Jeff Probst was surely long gone. He'd walked from my dream straight out of Brownsville, and back to Hollywood where he belongs, smiling all the way with oh–those dimples!

I stumbled my way to the coffeemaker, dumped the grounds and began a new pot. While it brewed, I decided that as I grew older, boring imaginary encounters like the one I just had would probably be the new normal for me. My "hot celebrity sex dreams" would become nothing more than "lame celebrity greeting dreams."

Coffee made, I poured a cup, then plopped myself down on the kitchen chair.

The old, tired, lumpy chair.

32
Five Crappy Cars

When shopping for vehicles, I really don't ask for much. If it's cheap, old and the check engine light is on, well then hey–I'll take it.

It sure seems that way, anyway. Look outside and you'll see one, two, three, four, five crappy cars, all with activated check engine lights. And five crappy cars minus four drivers equals what?

One driveway full of bad ideas, otherwise known as the Weber Fleet, which again consists of five vehicles for only the Husband, the Hobo, the Princess and I.

Please do not be jealous of these many and various cars; they're all in perpetual states of disrepair and have more than 100,000 miles. In fact, the odometer of White Wanda, the 2002 Honda CR-V, just flipped to 300,000 miles. We thought about throwing her a little party, but then the other CR-V, Black Betty, would be jealous, and we do not need that kind of discord in the driveway. They're all very busy out there. You know, breaking down and stuff.

As the youngest of the fleet, Black Betty hasn't malfunctioned much–yet. But being that the Husband and I both drive 90 miles a day for work–and the fact that we keep our cars for absolute decades–she's bound to start disintegrating soon.

Speaking of disintegration, walk with me–will you?–out to the crappy car lot and meet our team of misfits:

2008 Honda Civic

Coming in at a cool 210,000 miles, the Civic sits crumbling, rotting and living on borrowed time. It's black like Black Betty, or at least it was until its paint started peeling. Now she's as gray as your grandma and runs at the very same speed.

None of this is the Civic's fault, really. It is what is known as a "salvage vehicle," meaning it was totaled and technically belongs in the junkyard. Somebody somewhere rebuilt the Civic, and I purchased it from some Russians on craigslist. Now, normally "purchased" and "Russians" are words referring to nefarious actions of politicians, but that didn't stop me from driving to a sketchy part of Columbus to talk to some sketchy foreigners and pay them several thousand dollars for a sketchy car.

I met said Russians at a gas station on the city's southwest side. They couldn't speak English, so we used hand signals to communicate, and I walked around the Civic nodding and smiling, then ducked inside to check for the most important thing, which was, of course, a functioning radio. After some more smiling, nodding and walking around the car, I stopped and gave the Russians a thumbs up. This, as everyone knows, is the universal sign for "I am the moron who will buy your crappy car."

Despite its junkyard status, the Civic was a decent vehicle at first. It did a fine job hauling the kids and me around for several years—at least until I passed it on to the Husband. Then it began falling apart, largely due to what I call the Filth Factor.

The Filth Factor happens when a vehicle is never, ever cleaned and its owner cheerfully flings his discarded food, trash and who-knows-what around as though the car is his own personal landfill.

Observe if you will the stained seats, the disgusting carpet, the trash on the floor, the dust-covered dashboard. Feast your eyes upon the filthy cup holders, filled with crusty ketchup, petrified french fries, and what I sincerely hope are skin flakes and not boogers.

Because of the Husband-inflicted Filth Factor, the Civic now has low self-esteem, causing her to fall apart before our very eyes. The A/C blows hot air. The back of the driver's seat fell off, exposing her twisted, dusty innards. On the dash, the check engine light has been joined by every other available warning beacon, indicating that ALL the things are broken. And each day, another flake of black paint drifts hopelessly to the ground, as she waits in the driveway to die.

2002 Honda CR-V

Also waiting to die is White Wanda, whom you met earlier. She, too, came from craigslist. But instead of sketchy foreigners, I bought her from a dealer in 2005, which means she has been in our family forever, and by that I mean generations. I drove her, the Husband drove her and the Princess drove her all through high school. Wanda was very good to us for a very long time.

But Wanda is now 105 in dog years, and it's starting to show because thanks to her failing transmission, she can barely move. When she eventually gets going, she tops out at 50 m.p.h. and drinks gas as if it's Gatorade. At any given moment, Wanda is on the verge of a major, major breakdown.

Naturally, we felt this was a great time to pass her down from the Princess to the Hobo. He looks super studly driving his sweet soccer-mom mobile to school each day, sputtering down the road and knowing that Wanda is probably the reason he doesn't have a girlfriend yet. He calls Wanda a junker.

We prefer to call her birth control.

2003 Volkswagen Beetle convertible

To the left of Wanda is the Volkswagen Beetle, otherwise known as my bug, my money pit, and my great big midlife crisis.

This is actually my second Beetle because my first one caught fire and left me stranded on the side of the road. While waiting for the fire truck, I watched as my bug burned to the ground. Then, I made this solemn vow:

I must buy another one immediately.

So I hopped on craigslist yet again, searching and searching until I found my next bad idea: a 2003 cream-colored *convertible* Beetle.

Yes, a convertible. The irrational choice of sweaty menopausal women everywhere. How I would look! How I would live! How the wind would blow through my thinning middle-aged hair!

That's how I found myself driving five hours in what should have been a three-hour trip during the winter's worst snowstorm to purchase the convertible bug from a small used-car dealer in the mountains of Pennsylvania.

Mountains. Convertible. Used-car dealer. These are words that, when strung together, define the phrase "horrible idea." Add to that sentence the word "snowstorm" and you then have what is known as a "the day that I'll probably die."

Because this was not just any snowstorm. The snow fell so hard and so fast that the plow-drivers hadn't even bothered to come out, which led to five inches of snow on roads already as slick as snot from a previous ice storm. I grew up in the snow-belt, so I have tons of experience with bad roads. But this was some next-level shizz-nit, and let me tell you: I slid. I prayed.

I cried.

Still, I thought I'd be OK after picking up the car because I had what I thought was a genius plan: my sister-in-law lived about 20 minutes from the dealership, so I'd drive the bug to her place, spend the night and wait out the snowstorm.

Did I call her to discuss this? Did I make sure she'd be home? Did I give her any advance notice at all? I did not. I slid, prayed and cried all the way up the mountains, desperate to purchase my next bad idea.

Five heart-stopping, nerve-wracking, white-knuckle-gripping hours later, I pulled into the tiny dealership's snow-covered lot. The owner, with whom

I'd spoken on the phone, waved me inside through the window.

"Wow," he said. "I can't believe you drove all that way in this weather. You are crazy!"

I shook the snow off my coat. "And you are right."

"Hey—at least you made it," he said. "I put the Beetle in the garage, out of the weather."

He pointed to an open doorway, and there it was. My bug, my convertible, my very own midlife crisis. Cream-colored, black-topped, she was small, sassy and round, just like me.

Did I start the engine? Did I take it for a test drive? Did I peek under the hood and pretend to know what I was looking at?

Of course I didn't.

I did, however, clap my hands with glee. "I'll take it!"

The dealer smiled. "Wow," he said, which made me think, *Why does he keep saying wow?* "OK, so—I'll draw up the paperwork."

He handed me the key before turning back to his office. "Feel free to start it up."

Start it up I did. I was rewarded with the reassuring glow of the check engine light.

Look at that, I thought. *It's a sign!*

While the dealer worked on his computer, I stayed inside the car and dreamed of the awesome times I'd have in my new ride. Top-down trips around town. Top-down trips to the lake. Even a top-down trip to Walmart would be an adventure, though I knew that A) any trip to Walmart is an adventure, and B) top-down has a completely different meaning there.

The dealer interrupted my reverie with a stack of forms, which I happily signed without reading. I wrote a check and gave him the keys to my trade-in, then I hopped in the bug, adjusted the rearview mirrors and remembered the blizzard outside.

"Are you going to stay at a hotel or something?" asked the dealer. "Maybe wait out this snow?"

I shook my head. "Nah. My sister-in-law lives around here. I'll just stay with her."

"Wow," he said yet again. "OK, well, good luck!"

"Good luck!" is the last thing you want to hear from a used car salesman. But those were his last words to me, and I soon found out why because I wasn't even three minutes down the road before the car began what I can only describe as bucking like a freaking horse. And as you can imagine, bucking like a freaking horse doesn't mix well with icy roads. Every time the car bucked, it fishtailed, sliding either toward the berm or oncoming traffic.

I figured it was a transmission issue—you know, using my vast mechanical expertise—but instead of returning the car to the dealer and asking for a full refund, I drove on because I was in love. With a car.

Like an idiot.

After about 15 minutes of the bucking and sliding, I decided enough was enough and dialed my sister-in-law to ask her if I could crash–no pun intended–at her place. I called her house several times, but there was no answer. So I called her cell phone–no answer. Finally, I called her at work.

Still, no damn answer.

Beads of sweat began running down my temples. My heart lurched with each buck. The unrelenting snow dumped ever downward, and when the car wasn't fishtailing, the strong winds threatened to put it in the ditch anyway, and mind you–these were not little drainage ditches. They were steep, dangerous ditches off the sides of–and I cannot stress this enough–mountains. These were Road Runner/Wile E. Coyote ditches, also known as canyons, perfect for a convertible to roll down and land on its soft little top.

And my giant hard head.

I am probably going to die today, I thought.

I should have stopped at the nearest hotel, ran into a room and kissed the filthy carpeting, thankful to be alive. But I already felt guilty about the money I'd just spent on a car that I knew would need major repairs. The Husband wasn't going to be happy, and I didn't want to drop any more cash on my terrible decision.

So as is often the case in my life, one bad idea led to another, and I kept driving. I slid. I prayed. I cried.

Again.

I'd like to say that things got easier. I'd like to say the storm subsided a little bit. But it didn't, and on I went lurching through the endless whiteness. Aside from the snow, the ice, and the wind, the sliding, praying and crying, I don't remember much else from that day. I've probably blocked it from my mind.

All I know is that I lurched up the driveway in the dark, hours after I was expected. The Husband, who had been waiting for me, stood at the doorway.

"I can't believe you drove all that way in this weather. You are crazy."

"You are right," I said, tossing my purse on the couch.

"How do you like your car?" he asked. "How does it run?"

"I love it!" I said, avoiding further detail.

There was no sense telling him about the bug's problems. He found out a few weeks later when we paid $2,400 for transmission repair. And then six months after that when we paid $800 for computer problems. And five months after that when we paid $1,000 for a new exhaust system.

And this year when we paid $650 for electrical issues that still aren't resolved.

In spite of its constant state of disrepair, I am still in love. With a car. Like a moron.

And I still call her my bug, my baby, my great big midlife crisis. The Husband has many other names for her. But they are cuss words, and I won't repeat them here because I am a fucking lady.

2005 Chevrolet Silverado

Now, please turn your attention to the southwest corner of the Weber Crappy Car Lot. There you will find a Chevy Silverado Z71, a.k.a. the worst idea the Husband has ever had.

That's right. I may be the Queen of Bad Ideas, but the Husband has his fair share—at least in the realm of vehicles. And trust me. The Silverado was the worst possible idea ever.

I mean, that truck. Four-wheel drive, nice interior, white with silver trim—great-looking, yes, but it runs like a . . . never mind. It doesn't run at all. I call it the supermodel of pickup trucks: nice to look at, but otherwise pretty much worthless.

Like I said—I'm not that good at buying reliable vehicles. But at least the ones I purchase can usually be repaired. The Husband's Silverado has been in the shop at least nine times in the two years we've owned it, for various reasons ranging from ignition troubles to transmission problems to vague sensor issues that left the mechanic scratching his head and saying, "Hell, I don't know what's wrong with it," then handing us a $650 invoice for 28 hours of labor.

The Husband bought the truck on his own. He did not have my Helpful Guidance™ and vast mechanical expertise when he made this purchase, and so we ended up with a total and complete piece of shit. In case he forgets, I like to periodically remind him:

"This truck is a piece of shit!"

I've known it was a POS since the day he brought it up the driveway. Still, even though I've always been aware it was a hunk of junk, I once made the boneheaded decision to drive it anyway. All for the love of a couch.

A white couch.

As we've established, I adore white couches and now own several of them. But years ago, I didn't have any. This was a huge problem in my eyes, as I spent hours on Pinterest every morning drooling over living rooms with white couches. I somehow overlooked the fact that there were never any shedding black meth labs or big dirty mastiffs in these staged rooms, because, well, the couches just looked so pretty. So classy.

Unfortunately, they were also ridiculously expensive.

Enter my old friend IKEA. Thanks to my poor-girl past, I'm an avid bargain hunter and IKEA shopper, and I soon figured out that I didn't have to buy a $2,000 Pottery Barn white couch that the dogs would just destroy. Instead, I could buy a $399 white IKEA couch—that the dogs would just destroy.

So, when our federal income tax check came that spring, I repeated my annual tradition of cashing it before the Husband even knew it was there. Then I hatched a plan.

A really bad plan.

Possibly the world's worst plan.

Drive to IKEA in the Husband's jacked-up pickup truck and buy a white couch! I thought.

It will be OK! I thought.

Ha ha ha!

Sob

The things I will do for a white couch.

Let's see. POS Chevy–check. Six hours round-trip–check. Self-serve furniture store–check. Two hundred pound sofa–check.

All by myself–check.

After making this series of terrible decisions, I woke up early one cloudy spring morning and packed nothing but a large bottle of water, my purse and my $399. I walked out the door and to the truck warily, the way one would approach a bomb.

I tried to comfort myself with the fact that it had just come back from the shop after yet another repair.

It's just been fixed! I thought.

It will be OK! I thought.

And off I went, bouncing down the driveway.

That's right. Bouncing. The truck had just had an alignment and some new tires installed, but one of its current major problems was some kind of issue that left the driver bopping down the road as if driving on four basketballs, only bouncier.

I'd known about the bouncing and had driven around town with it with no major issues. But bouncing around Brownsville at 35 m.p.h. was one thing; bouncing across I-70 at faster speeds was quite another. Anything above 65 m.p.h. made the bouncing and shimmying unmanageable. So I poked along in the slow lane at 62, and oh, how I bounced. How I sweated. How I cussed.

Around noon, I became incredibly hungry. I also had to pee, which was no surprise because if I'm breathing, I have to pee. But I wouldn't stop for any of it, as I knew that if I did so, I might not start again.

You do not tarry with basic needs when driving a POS Chevy.

The Husband, not a fan of IKEA or spending money in general, had stayed behind to watch the kids. Since he wasn't around for the joy of this trip, I decided to call him up and give him my valuable opinion.

"Hello?" he said.

"This truck is a piece of shit!"

"I know, dear. You've mentioned it."

"That is all."

Click

I hung up on him so that I could better focus on bouncing, sweating and cussing. I used my time in the slow lane to project rage onto everything and everyone in my sight, glaring at the RVs, the Buicks, the turtles on the side of the road as they passed me.

After many days, hours, years, it seemed, the basketballs and I thumped thankfully into the Cincinnati IKEA parking lot, right along with what appeared to be the entire state of Ohio. And Indiana.

And most of Kentucky.

Apparently, the people of the Midwest–and part of the south–had also received their federal income tax refunds that week, and decided on a fun day of seething humanity and cheap Scandinavian furniture.

I grabbed one of the last available parking spots and rushed inside. I walked with the herd to the sales floor, where I joined the rest of the tri-state area as they trudged like dead-eyed zombies through a store as big as an airport.

Because of my harrowing trip down the interstate, I didn't have much energy to deal with the throngs of people crowding every inch of available space. Babies crying, kids whining, elderly folks stopping in the middle of the aisles–IKEA is set up like a huge maze constantly clogged with human traffic, and there aren't many shortcuts. If you don't know where you're going–and I didn't–you have to snake through the entire mammoth building to your eventual goal: the warehouse section and cheap Scandinavian furniture in boxes.

Big boxes.

Very big boxes.

I finally arrived in the warehouse and stared open-mouthed at my chosen white couch, the Ektorp, inside its gargantuan carton. The physics alone were frightening: I am 5'2" and weigh, well, none of your business, but the box looked to be roughly twice my size on both counts, and I wondered how in the world I was supposed to get it from the shelf to the cart without flattening myself like an ant.

In true self-serve IKEA fashion, employees were nowhere around. As I stood and contemplated the big box o' sofa, an old, stooped woman paused beside me.

"You need some help with that, honey?"

I turned and eyed my fellow customer: white-haired, frail, a couple inches shorter than me. I sincerely doubted her couch-lifting abilities, but I was desperate.

"Um, yeah–but are you sure?"

I should not have doubted.

She whipped my cart to the front of the box, wedged it underneath, stood aside and pushed the sofa down with a flick of her wrinkly wrist. The carton landed with a thump, stable and ready to roll.

"Wow, thanks!" I said. "That was just . . . amazing."

She shrugged. "That's how you do it. Just flip it down."

Couch on the cart, I thanked her again and re-joined the populations of Ohio, Indiana and Kentucky at the registers, where we waited oh, four or five hours to check out? I don't know.

Time has no meaning at IKEA.

I should have taken a nap. By the time I paid and wrestled the box into the pickup, I was once again exhausted.

And I had a bigger issue.

The carton, too long for the bed of the truck, tilted up and rested on the closed tailgate. That wouldn't have been a problem except that our particular tailgate latch was, you guessed it, broken and given to popping open at the slightest pressure. I had no rope to secure anything, and again no help as there were no stock boys and I couldn't find the old lady anywhere.

I stared at the box resting on the broken tailgate and said a silent prayer. Then, I hopped in the cab, started the engine and shimmied onto the freeway, anticipating the worst.

Back onto the interstate I bounced, 62 m.p.h., my eyes flipping maniacally between the windshield and the rearview mirror. I fully expected the shuddering tailgate to collapse at any time, my hard-won cheap white couch crushing cars Godzilla-like as it careened to the side of the road.

I bounced, I sweated, and I cussed.

Hours went by in this way. I grew hungry again. I had to pee, again. And turtles and Buicks passed me. Again.

It was time once more to give my valuable opinion. I dialed the Husband, who picked up his phone without saying hello.

"I know, dear. You've mentioned it."

Click

I have no idea why he hung up on me, but I didn't have time to think about it. I drove on, and eventually, finally, amazingly, the decades passed. I made it home, bouncing up the driveway at 8 p.m. Angry and spent, I rushed into the house, shouted, "Never again!" and pushed the children down on the way to the bathroom.

Never again indeed. I had been to IKEA before, but not alone, not for a large couch, and definitely not in a POS Chevy. It was a harrowing, epic journey in three or four parts, a terrifying odyssey I will not repeat.

So please, friends, by all means learn from my mistakes, and mark my words. A trip to IKEA requires strategy, patience, fortitude and preferably, Xanax. Before you go, make sure that you rest up. Eat something. Pee often. Bring along some sort of strong male—or an old, stooped woman—then ride shotgun and get drunk.

All the better.

And for the love of God and cheap Scandinavian furniture, please, I beseech you: Take a functioning pickup truck. Do not borrow ours.

Because I don't know if I've mentioned it, but that truck is a piece of shit.

33
Warning: Acronyms Ahead

Welcome to Ohio. Don't be an asshole.

That's not our state motto, but it should be. Because for the most part, Ohioans are known for being nice. For being polite. For being friendly.

Of course we have our faults. We can be stubborn, backward and many of us are pessimists, or as we prefer to call it–realists. Positive thinking? You're in the wrong state.

Realistic thinking? Come, young grasshopper. Sit by us.

Buckeyes really don't expect much out of life. A job, a place to live, a little family to call our own–that's about all we require to make it through our 80-odd years. See, things aren't always easy here. What with our struggling farms, Rust-Belt cities and six-month winters, we deal with constant uncertainty and we know that at any time, jobs could disappear. Crops could fail.

Cows could die.

That's why Ohioans are tough, resilient and unfailingly practical. We hope for the best but are always prepared for the inevitable worst. We know that the path to contentment is low expectations and standards, or as I like to call it, the "Low Expectations and Standards System," otherwise known as LESS. Its message is simple: keep your expectations and standards low, low, low.

I bet you've heard this a thousand times: Have hope! Chin up! Things will turn around.

But verily, I say unto you: Have no hope. Head down and power through. Things could remain the same, but likely will go straight down the shitter.

So in Ohio, we pride ourselves on low expectations, on LESS. Better to stay realistic than get disappointed when things don't go our way.

And you know what? We're good to each other precisely because we've been through a lot. We don't expect much, but if there's one thing most Ohioans *do* expect, it's decency and good manners from others. Life is unpredictable and hard enough. Why be a jerk? Might as well be kind. Work, work some more, pay the bills and, if you're lucky, maybe take a vacation once a year.

My family took a vacation recently, and it was here we once again encountered a type of person I call the MOWL, which stands for, you guessed it, Mean Old White Lady.

That's right–MOWL. Looks a lot like "MEOW," doesn't it? Not a coincidence.

Before anyone gets their granny panties in a bunch, let it be known that the MOWL is an exception, not a rule. There are plenty of Nice Old White Ladies–NOWLs–and plenty of garden-variety Old White Ladies, or OWLs.

But MOWLs are different creatures. They flock to the coast like the crabby old cats they are and move into beautiful houses, right on the beach. We saw them in restaurants, hissing at the wait staff. We saw them in grocery stores, growling at their husbands.

We saw them everywhere, scowling at us.

They're quite a shock to our Midwestern systems. We don't know quite what to make of all that . . . *anger*.

In one of my Mean Old White Lady run-ins, I walked up to the door of a department store and pulled the handle to enter. A MOWL immediately plowed through the other side, nearly knocking me down as she whisked out the door that I'd unknowingly held open especially for her.

I didn't really mind holding the door. But what did I get in return? Absolutely nothing. Of course not. But I'm from Ohio, so I expected something. *Where is my thank you?* I thought, *WHERE IS MY THANK YOU?!*

But "Thank you" is a phrase MOWLs don't know. Other words unfamiliar to them include "please," "hello" and "excuse me."

Later that week, I was shopping at the supermarket when I was forced to a stop by a MOWL. Wearing head-to-toe Lilly Pulitzer, the cheery colors completely at odds with her dark demeanor, she stood dead-center in the canned goods section with her cart blocking the entire aisle as she perused the label on a can of beans.

"Excuse me," I said.

Crickets

Thinking she might have been a little hard of hearing, I spoke louder.

"'Scuse me!" I said genially, adding a big Ohio smile.

Nothing. She didn't even look up from the can.

Obviously, she was completely deaf. I was going to have to get her attention somehow, so I edged closer to her cart, walked up beside her and waved.

"Hi there!" I said. "Could you excuse me, please? I'm just trying to get through."

She raised her haughty chin and glared at me over her glasses. "I heard you the first time," she hissed.

"Oh . . . I'm so sorry!" I stuttered, feeling like a jerk for no reason at all.

She huffed and moved her cart approximately 1.5 inches. I sucked in my gut and squeezed through, scraping the entire right side of my body across the edge of the shelves.

Bleeding from the arm, I said, "Thank you!" Then, unable to stop my dumb Ohio mouth, I added, "Have a good day!"

She scowled and went back to her beans.

Where is my 'You too!' I thought. *WHERE IS MY 'YOU TOO!'?*

It was a bad idea to talk to her at all. I knew better. I encounter the MOWLs every year on vacation; I've studied their actions, observed their rudeness, and I know it's best not to talk to them, even if they're in the way. They thrive on making others as miserable as they are, and attempting kindness—or even basic human interaction—sets them off.

Now, I hate to perpetuate a stereotype, so I'll just make a sweeping generalization and say that most MOWLs I observe seem to be from (*cough* like, Boston or something *cough*) places other than Ohio. I can tell by their accent and the noticeable lack of Rs as they speak, as in "Christ, Bahb, wheah did you pahk de cah?" Which of course in Ohio means, "Christ, Bob, where did you park the car?"

I have no idea why these women are so crabby. Could it be their doting husbands? Their designer clothes? Their beautiful homes in even more beautiful places?

Oh, so vexing to be wealthy and carefree.

Listen. I'm not naive. I know that I'm heading well into Old White Lady territory myself. Indeed I am lurching toward decrepitude at an alarming rate, and I've thoroughly documented it in this book, my last book and my blog, for the last 11 years. Failing eyesight. Wrinkling face. New chins every year. Boobs heading south faster than an SUV full of spring-break teenagers. For sure, gravity is pulling me down and underground soon enough and there isn't a day that goes by that I'm not made aware of my own waning mortality.

But that doesn't give me, or any other old woman, an excuse to be nasty. To be a MOWL.

As I've mentioned a time or six, I'm retiring soon, and I plan to spend my winters on the coast. I guess I'll have to get used to the MOWLs, as they're everywhere down there. I hope I don't become one of them, bitching and moaning and clogging up the canned goods.

I plan to just be an OWL. An owl who can kick some catty old MOWL ass if need be.

To survive, I'll probably have to learn some of their ways, to dish out the meanness they serve so freely unto me and everyone else around them.

When I see a scowling MOWL plowing out a door, I will *not* hold it open.

When an unresponsive MOWL blocks the aisle, I shall *bump* her cart.

Lightly, of course. I'm not a monster.

Sure, these rude actions will hurt my dopey Ohio heart, but they will not kill me. You can't break a Buckeye.

And after I make my point, I'll continue on my way and return my soul to its own sweet center. It's only right.

Because come on, man. Why be an asshole?

34
The Flaming Fairmont of Death

She was smokin' hot, and not in a good way.

Her vents spewed blue smoke and toxic electrical fumes. I tried to figure out how to make it across three lanes of Columbus rush hour traffic while maintaining bladder control.

Holy shit, I thought. *My car is on fire. Again.*

I shot across I-70 to the berm, grabbed my purse and jumped out of my car, a 1999 Volkswagen Beetle. I walked a few hundred yards down the shoulder, dialed 911, and watched as my car destroyed itself.

The situation was distressing but not surprising because so many of my terrible decisions seem to have motors. And engine problems. And serious safety issues.

In addition, this wasn't even my first car fire. That's right. I seem to have an affinity for really hot cars. Hot as in smoking. Hot as in danger. Hot as in FLAMES.

While standing on the shoulder waiting for the fire department, I pondered my horrible hot luck. *At least I got some warning this time*, I thought, unlike my first car fire. I have never, before or since, known a vehicle so intent on killing its driver, which is why I called it the Flaming Fairmont of Death.

To be clear, the FFOD was my first car. But as you know from "Go Ahead. Throw the Book at Me," my first *vehicle* was a Ford Ranger. A great ride, that truck–one that took me to ALL the parties and never caught fire even once. I fancied myself pretty awesome in my little grandpa truck. Until I managed to wreck it. Three times. In two years.

Driving skills. I had them.

Thanks to my many accidents, the insurance premium for the Ranger grew to an astronomical rate, so my mother was kind enough to sell me her piece of shit 1982 Ford Fairmont. I wasn't happy about it, but I needed something to get me to the parties.

Also, the radio worked.

The first time the FFOD tried to kill me, the police had pulled me over yet again. I was 19. Getting pulled over was kind of a job of mine.

"What did I do, officer?" I asked, cranking down my window. Cranking down windows was a thing we did in the 80s. "I wasn't speeding."

The cop lowered his chin and raised his eyebrows. "Miss," he said, "there are flames shooting out of your muffler."

"What do you mean?" I said.

He motioned with his finger. "Follow me."

I opened the door, walked back and peeked with him under the car. Sure enough, small blue flames blazed from the tailpipe.

"Wow," I said, clearly not grasping the gravity of the situation. "OK, I'll have that looked at as soon as I get some money."

Again, I was 19. Poverty was also kind of a job of mine.

The officer shook his head. "No. You'll call a tow truck *now*. The car isn't safe. You're not driving it home."

This worried me, but only because I was broke. The fact that I was more concerned about paying for a tow truck than by flames shooting out of my car just attests to my stupidity. But like I said: broke.

"I don't have any money for a tow truck!" I said.

The cop shrugged and turned away. "Do you have a credit card? You can use that."

I only liked to use my credit card for Very Important Things, such as Pitchers of Beer. But Officer Buzz Kill didn't give me much choice. With my Discover card, I paid to have the car towed back home, with strict orders from Buzz Kill not to operate it until I had the exhaust fixed.

Did I mention I had no money?

Anyway, I didn't see a problem. Various boys were consulted, and we– the brain-trust–figured mufflers were meant to be hot. As little penniless Rust-Belt ragamuffins, we each drove various pieces of shit that spewed smoke, gasoline, metal–all kinds of toxic matter, really–onto the street and/or unsuspecting pedestrians. So we figured my toasty little muffler was no big deal.

"Perfectly normal!" we said. "No reason to worry!"

That is how it came to pass that I ignored Buzz Kill's warning and kept driving my four-door blast furnace everywhere, cheating death and ignoring the polluted stink underneath.

You can't hurt me, Flaming Fairmont of Death. I laugh at your blue muffler flames!

Until one evening when driving home from class, I noticed a stronger than usual stench. I looked in the rear-view mirror to find nothing but smoke.

The backseat was on fire.

I slammed it into park, ran to a pay-phone and called my boyfriend at the time, who quickly raced to me and somehow ripped out the burning seat before the whole car engulfed.

Now I had no backseat. And obviously, it was time to get the exhaust system fixed.

Did I mention I was broke?

Anyway, the Flaming Fairmont of Death still ran fine. You could literally fry an egg on the metal under the missing seat. I know because I tried. As long as no flammable objects got placed on this metal, really–what was the harm?

Also, the radio worked.

So it was that your little idiotic friend here began driving around with two or three gallon jugs full of water. Whenever I smelled smoke, I'd simply pull over and pour water on the hot metal.

That'll cool her down! You're foiled again, FFOD!

My big jugs (see what I did there?) also came in handy a few months later, when the Fairmont Of Death's radiator started springing leaks. Anytime I saw smoke coming from the front of the car, I simply refilled the radiator with my handy-dandy jugs, and went on my way.

Engine fire, exhaust fire–I had it covered. After all, who needs an extinguisher when you have Aquafina?

These days, I look back and can't believe I drove that thing around, spewing smoke from both ends like the hideous ticking time bomb it was. I really should've chosen to bust out my beleaguered Discover card and have it fixed, but again: back then, me + credit card = Pitchers of Beer.

Like I said, I was 19. Poor choices were kind of a job of mine.

The fire truck's siren knocked me out of my Decade of Dumb and back to the current situation, standing on the side of another road watching yet another car burn. I had just started to grasp the horrific-yet-hilarious irony of it all when the firemen hopped out, grabbed their gear and extinguished the flames. One of them walked over to ask if I was OK.

"I'm fine," I said, laughing hysterically. "Haha–you know. Just another car fire!"

He stared at me quizzically, then shook his head and radioed a tow truck. Eventually a police officer–a nice one, unlike Buzz Kill–arrived and offered to give me a ride, so I jumped in the back of his cruiser and called it a damn day.

I had no idea what caused that second fire; I never would find out. But I did know one thing: I was still alive. Hey–if I could make it through my idiotic, poverty-filled youth, I could get through anything.

In the cruiser's backseat, I craned my neck to get one last glimpse of the smoky heap of rubble that had been my car. The officer signaled, accelerated and eased onto the interstate as I turned back around and smiled.

You can't hurt me, Flaming Fairmont of Death!
I laugh at your blue muffler flames!

35
Lost Identity: A Tale in Three Parts

The mall. A Kid Rock concert. The bottom of a clear, blue river.

You would think such places would have nothing in common. That they're just some arbitrary locations, or maybe a nightmare involving rivers, malls and washed-up rock stars. I've had stranger dreams.

But folks, I'm here to tell you that these places are absolutely related. Never underestimate my weird, random life or propensity for monumentally poor decisions. Because the mall, a Kid Rock concert and the bottom of a river are all places where, thanks to various bad ideas, I have lost my driver's license.

Please understand—I didn't lose my ID in three separate decades because of any criminal activity, rather the losses were all due to my own stupidity, and the cops weren't involved at all.

Except for sort of. This one time. But I'm sure you don't want to hear about that. It's ancient history. Plus, it was one of my most embarrassing moments.

Really? You still want to hear?

Oh, jeez. Alright.

It was the summer of 1987. A group of friends and I had decided to go to the Southern Park Mall in Boardman Ohio, because that was a big night out in 1987. I'm not sure what we actually *did* at the mall, as we were far too broke to shop or purchase food. Mostly we just walked around the mall *not* shopping and *not* eating. You know, as one does.

Or does not.

I had driven all of us there in my 1982 Ford Fairmont. You may remember this car from last chapter as the Flaming Fairmont of Death. But in 1987, it hadn't yet caught fire—although with its frequent breakdowns and extremely hot exhaust system, it was well on its way.

At least six of us had piled into the Fairmont, maybe more, because I had made the really bad decision to cram as many people as possible in for a Big Night Out at the Mall. I can't remember everyone who was along for the ride, but I'm pretty sure the cast included my BFF Amber, as well as the King of Bad Ideas, Mark Planey.

Now, I may be the Queen of Bad Ideas, but some of Mark Planey's ideas make me look like a Rhodes Scholar. Plus, he takes no shame in being the King of Bad Ideas. In fact, if you met him, he'd probably tell you, "I am the King of Bad Ideas!" He had one of his worst ideas that night in 1987, which is how the police got involved.

But first, I lost my driver's license.

I lost my license because I'd piled six 18-year-olds in a car that was only meant for four people. The Fairmont had bench seats, so three of us crammed together in the front and three in the back with little room to spare. Since I couldn't put my purse in the middle of the front seat as usual, I made the brilliant choice to put it to my left, between my body and the door. And what happens to something that's between one's body and the car door when said door opens?

Exactly. It falls out.

Which is precisely what happened the night I opened my door in the parking lot of the Southern Park Mall.

I didn't discover the missing purse until we'd left the mall and gone to McDonald's to pool our spare change for pop. We sped back to the mall and asked every security guard we could find if someone had turned in a purse, but unfortunately, it was nowhere to be found.

I was deeply upset at this turn of events. Not that my purse contained much–see info re: broke-ass teenager above–but it did hold my license and *cough* a fake ID *cough.*

My friends, still in possession of their own purses and wallets, were quite joyous and carefree as I pulled out of the lot for a second time. I began dejectedly driving back to our hometown while they laughed, yelled, blared the radio and otherwise ignored my bottomless sadness at the loss of my most valuable possession–my fake ID.

So great was their happiness and raucousness as we approached the exit ramp of I-680 that Mark Planey, in his infinite wisdom, decided we should do a Chinese Fire Drill, wherein vehicle occupants jump out of the car at an intersection, run around the car, and get back in different seats.

Although I was excellent at bad ideas, as the driver, I did not approve of this one. I voiced concerns about any impending Chinese Fire Drill, and anyone getting out of the car in general.

"That's a bad idea!" I said.

But they would not be stopped.

And so it came to pass that as I rolled to a stop at the end of the Western Reserve Road exit, five unruly teens jumped out, ran around my car and launched themselves back inside to different seats. Hilarity ensued. They laughed and laughed.

I was not amused. Still mourning my purse, I shook my head, eased off the ramp and back into traffic, thankful that among the many vehicles in my rear-view mirror, I didn't see a police cruiser.

As you know from reading this far, the only luck I have is of the bad variety. So guess who did end up seeing us? Guess who followed us back to town? Guess who was an off-duty police officer and used his CB radio to contact his fellow officers?

I don't remember the off-duty officer's name. I've blocked it from my mind, the way people do after traumatic events. All I know is as I turned right onto route 170 from Western Reserve Road, the entire police force of New Middletown, Ohio, sat in the village's only shopping plaza.

We thought it was a murder scene. How else to explain no less than four cruisers gathered in a semi-circle, lights flashing, on a small-town Saturday night?

"What's going on?" asked Amber.

"Someone must've been shot," said Mark.

But no one had died. No, the fine officers of the entire police force of New Middletown, Ohio were waiting for us, which we soon realized when one of the cruisers left the others, sped out of the parking lot, and, siren screaming, pulled us to the side of the road.

"What the hell?" said Amber.

"Here we go!" said Mark.

The other three cruisers swarmed us as I pulled the Fairmont over. One by one, we were removed from the vehicle and questioned, yelled at and otherwise harassed by the officers, all thanks to Mark Planey's Really Bad Idea, a.k.a. the Chinese Fire Drill that had happened nearly two towns away.

I burst into tears. The cop yelling at me was especially brutal, and insisted his off-duty buddy had said that during the infamous fire drill I'd gotten out of the car, too, when I most certainly had not.

Compounding the whole mess was the fact that I'd lost my purse, so I didn't have an ID to give to Officer Asshole. After berating me for a good 20 minutes, he directed me, still sobbing, into the back of his cruiser while he and the other men dealt with the rest of the hardened criminals in the Fairmont.

For a solid hour, the questioning, berating, etc., continued with the other derelicts, and my car was thoroughly searched. Finding nothing, the police eventually decided–rightfully, I might add–that as much as they wanted to, they couldn't take us to jail because we hadn't committed our heinous crime in their jurisdiction. After giving me a pricey ticket for not having my license, they finally let us go.

It was an unforgettable, harrowing event, one that led me to dislike and avoid police officers for quite some time.

Until I married one. Then had two of his kids.

I learned my lesson, though, and from then on, I *always* carried my license with me.

You know, until I lost it the next time.

Kid Rock concerts are not known for good decisions. No. Drugs, nudity, live sex shows–these are your general Kid Rock options.

But instead of engaging in any of those poor choices, I made a different bad decision at a Kid Rock show: I stuffed my driver's license in the back pocket of my jeans.

This was a decade or more after the Great Chinese Fire Drill Incident of 1987, but I was still scarred from Officer Asshole, so I always made sure to carry my ID with me. Plus, I knew I'd want to purchase a horrible $20 concert beer.

Or two.

Upon arriving at the show, I did just that. I walked to the beer stand, grabbed my license and my money from my back pocket, and showed my ID to the bartender when she requested it. I completed the transaction and took my horrible $20 beer to my seat.

I sipped it slowly, trying to make it last. Lines for horrible concert beer are notoriously long. You can miss half the show–hell, half your life–waiting to fork over the equivalent of a small car payment for a plastic cup of piss water.

As a trained horrible beer-drinking professional, I timed it perfectly and finished the last of it just as the first act ended. I left the Husband in our seats and walked back to the stand to stake my place in the long, long line, where time stood still, days went by and years passed. Finally, just as Kid Rock was about to come on stage, it was my turn to step up to the counter.

"One Budweiser, please," I said.

This time, the bartender didn't card me. "Twenty dollars."

I pulled the cash from my pocket . . .

. . . and promptly launched my license onto the ground.

Which I didn't notice. Nope. Not at all.

Until the next day, when I dug through my pants and found nothing but a ticket stub, some dryer lint and a pocket full of regret.

The worst part of it all was the photo on the front of that particular ID was the best I'd ever taken. I looked rested, young and only one of my several chins was showing–a miracle in itself.

Also, as the Husband pointed out, "You literally just got that license three weeks ago."

He was right. I'd just replaced my previous ID, which had expired. So back I went to the dreaded DMV, where I got the next license I swore I'd never lose.

And I didn't.

For a while.

Many license-filled years went by. I grew wiser, and I grew older. Much, much older. You'd think I had learned my lesson.

But you'd be wrong.

I am still an idiot, as evidenced by my most recent ID loss at the bottom of a river a few weeks ago while kayaking with the Hobo in Weeki Wachee Springs, Florida.

Even though it stole my license and tried very hard to kill me, I have to say: Weeki Wachee is beautiful, and not to be missed. It was located 2.5 hours away from where the Hobo and I had been staying, but I decided it would be worth the drive, because, like I say, clear, blue and gorgeous.

I made reservations for the kayak trip in advance, and the Hobo and I got up at the absolute crack of dawn and drove north to the launch site. We parked and gathered our things: water bottles, sunscreen, and–pay attention because this becomes important–my brand-new phone inside a waterproof phone bag.

Now, I always use a waterproof phone bag when kayaking. But the bag was even more crucial for this trip because my phone was exactly one day old, and as you know if you read my last book, I have a history when it comes to phones and water.

Although there was vodka involved that time.

There was no alcohol in sight when I put my new iPhone in the phone bag and hung it by its cord around my neck. Figuring I'd need it to check in at the kayak launch, I then made what I thought was a brilliant decision: I'd put my driver's license in the waterproof phone bag so I could leave my purse safely locked in the car.

What a great idea! I thought.

I'm so smart! I thought.

Ha ha ha! Hindsight is not only 20/20. It's funny as hell.

Now that the whole thing's over.

Anywho.

We checked in with park staff, grabbed our life jackets and kayaks, and launched into a river that was, as promised, absolutely beautiful. Crystal clear and white-bottomed, it was like kayaking in a natural swimming pool, if said pool had huge snakes, giant spiders and freaking ALLIGATORS, all of which we saw lining the shore.

Despite the many dangers, I treasured my time with the Hobo. He really seemed to enjoy the trip, and at 17, he doesn't get excited by anything anymore, nor does he really want to spend much time with me. To record this momentous occasion, I decided that we needed to take a picture together in the kayak.

I held up the phone bag, and soon discovered that my new phone was too big to take a picture from inside the bag. While the clear plastic in the middle protected the iPhone from water and would allow a smaller phone to take a photo, the black border around the edges blocked my new, larger phone's camera lens. I'd have to take it out of the bag, a scary proposition due to my dubious water/phone history. But the fact that the Hobo was actually *smiling* while *gasp* *spending time with me* was too important to miss, and needed to be documented. I had to do it.

So I carefully opened the phone bag, carefully reached in, carefully withdrew my phone . . .

. . . and flung my driver's license directly into the water.

In my haste, I'd forgotten my license had been tightly packed into the bag behind the phone. I watched in horror as it sailed in slow motion away from the boat and into the river, where it sank to the sandy bottom.

At first, the Hobo and I were too dumbfounded to say anything. I leaned over the edge of the kayak and barely saw the outline of the license in the sand below.

"I bet I could swim down and get it," I said.

The Hobo wasn't sure. "I don't know, Mom. That looks like a bad idea."

"Nah. The water's clear; the bottom doesn't look very deep. Let's pull the kayak up to the shore there, and I'll jump in."

Hindsight again. So funny. I crack myself up.

We paddled to the shore, and the Hobo grabbed a tree branch to steady the boat while I prepared to get out. I took off my life jacket and jumped into the crystal clear water.

Where I was immediately swept 40 feet downstream.

"Jeez!" I said, flailing my arms.

"Are you alright?" yelled the Hobo.

I tried to remain calm. "Yeah. I'm just going to try to swim back that way again and find it."

Fighting the current, saying a silent prayer, I swam as hard as I could toward the kayak and what I hoped was my license. I sank underwater, struggled to the bottom and immediately got swept downstream again.

"Mom!" yelled the Hobo as my head broke the water's surface.

"I'm OK!" I said, lying.

"I really don't think this is a good idea!"

I responded with my two least favorite words. "You're right!"

I struggled to the shore 10 yards down from the Hobo, where I grabbed a tree branch. "Try to come and get me!"

The Hobo released his branch and did as he was told, paddling south to where I clung for life from my own tree. He pulled up and steadied the kayak.

I grabbed the side of the boat, swung my legs down onto the shore . . .

. . . and immediately sank into two feet of quicksand.

A word about quicksand: I'd always been under the impression that it doesn't really exist, that it was only something from *Gilligan's Island* or a Road Runner cartoon. But I'm here to tell you quicksand is real, and it's yet another way Florida will try to kill you.

While sinking in the muck, I tried not to think about the giant spider, large snake, or the ALLIGATOR we'd seen not ten minutes before on the shore where I now flailed around. The more I struggled, the more the quicksand pulled me down. As I sank, I said the smartest thing I'd said all day.

"This was a really bad idea."

Several terrifying minutes went by, but finally, my feet found something hard under the quicksand. It might have been a rock. It might have been a tree root.

It might very well have been an alligator. At that point, I didn't care.

I pushed forcefully on whatever it was with both feet and hoisted myself into the kayak, where the Hobo held us steady.

"Are you OK?" he asked.

I peered down into the depths of the water where, if I squinted, I could just make out my license.

It seemed so easy, so close, to reach down and get it. But the water's clarity was deceiving. As I'd just found out, it rested at least 10 feet down in a strong underwater current.

The edges of the ID shone in the rippling water. It looked beautiful. It looked shimmery.

It looked like it would be there for a long, long time.

"Yeah, I'm OK," I told the Hobo. "Let's just go."

We paddled down the river, and I left myself behind.

Again.

36
Useful as Well as Ornamental

There are bookshelves, floating shelves, corner shelves, and elves on shelves.

Then, there is my Shelf.

It's something to see, I tell you what. Older than the Nixon administration! Stronger than a half-ton truck! Able to calm screaming toddlers with a single squeeze! Look–here on my chest! It's deflated balloons! It's a pair of bowling pins! No, wait!

It's just . . .

my Shelf.

And when I say Shelf, I refer to my mammies, my milkers, my honkers, my orbs. My chi-chis, my bouncers, my buoys and my baby bar.

I refer, of course, to my boobs.

It's time to give them the respect they deserve. They've seen better decades, for sure, such as the 80s and some of the 90s. But still, the big gulps have been useful as well as relatively ornamental since 1982, when they poked through my torso like a couple of rocks.

Really painful rocks.

Since then, Barnes & Noble have been through it all: the sports bra. The training bra. The underwire bra. All bras in general.

They've also known an enthusiastic male or two–possibly three . . .

Shut up. Who's counting?

As those things go, one extremely enthusiastic male became the biggest fan of the Shelf. Nary a day went by when he wasn't ogling, patting, fondling, squeezing, or otherwise molesting the sweater puppies.

One thing led to another, which led, as it does, to a pregnancy, a baby, then another pregnancy, and another baby, all of which caused many changes for my lady lumps. Up, down, big, little. Sore, chafed, dry, wet.

Still, they survived. A little older now, a little lower, but still–here.

Once, they were Mary Kate and Ashley. Now they are more Lucy and Ethel. No, they ain't what they used to be. But, I ask you, who among us is?

Over the years I've developed many other uses for the milk duds, the main one being simply: the Shelf.

That's right. Who needs a corner shelf, a bookshelf, a floating shelf, or any other shelf when a gal can use the handy-dandy ledge she carries around with her at all times anyway? Foods, drinks, books, gadgets. Why, any kind of item is available and ready, simply by employing the weapons of mass distraction.

I use my particular Shelf for any number of things. It comes in especially handy in the bathroom, where, in combination with a bra, one can store one's phone whilst settling oneself on the toilet.

True, sitting on the toilet with a phone shouldn't be a difficult thing. However, I managed to make it so on three separate occasions when my handset fell out of my back pocket and straight into the bowl.

After a lot of cussing and a few new phones, I learned that a quick stuff into the bra and onto the Shelf before sitting prevents unfortunate phone plops. When settled, one can pull out one's device and have a nice relaxing Twitterfest.

Just like the current president.

That's not the only electronic use for the Shelf–it also makes a handy ledge for an iPad. The Shelf is particularly helpful in the bathtub, where, as everyone knows, one must surf the internet while soaking. Because really– what's a nice warm bath without cat videos? Not much. Not much at all.

The Shelf has been many things to many people. My children, for instance, viewed it as their own personal tissue box, and from birth to age 3, each deposited great gobs of spit, snot, food and even vomit on the Shelf. The Hobo was especially a fan of rubbing his face on it, sighing deeply as he wiped his face from side to side.

"Mmm, boobies," he said. "I like boobies!"

Yes, the Shelf has had many enthusiasts and served many functions over the years. But no one has enjoyed its uses more than I, especially in the realm of food and beverage storage. Eating a hamburger but getting full? Save a little ketchup for later! Craving a salad but out of dressing? Have some ranch left over from lunch! Why, any number of condiments and sauces can be stored upon the Shelf, as evidenced by every single shirt in my closet.

The Husband tries to help. Whether we're sitting at the kitchen table or out at a restaurant, he likes to keep a close eye on it. He's thoughtful like that.

"Watch your Shelf!" he says, as food drips off my face and down my neck. "WATCH YOUR SHELF!"

At that point, I lean forward, but it's always too late. I'll forget about the incident and, like a nincompoop, neglect to spray the stain before throwing the blouse into the hamper. The grease then seeps into the fabric despite my best efforts and repeated washings. I hang the shirt in the closet, where it dies a slow death among its many stained brethren.

Now, I could blame the bazooms for this. But how can I get mad when the Shelf is so functional? It's a great place to balance a glass of wine! It's a fine site to cradle a can of beer!

It's the perfect place to prop a plate of chicken wings!

Let's not forget the snacks. Running around and know you'll be hungry later? Stuff some string cheese for the road. Kids getting hangry while shopping? Whip out the granola bar you packed before you left. Don't risk putting food in your purse where it will get crushed, lost, or tossed. Cheetos, Doritos, Tostitos and more can sit safely upon the Shelf. Indeed, after certain late and debaucherous evenings, I've awakened to find a half-dozen Cheez-Its resting comfortably inside my tank top.

Now you might call that sloppy. But I call it breakfast.

So, Women of America, hear me when I speak.

Never underestimate the power of the jubblies, the cupcakes, the chesticles, the thunder jugs.

The nubbers, the gunners, the milk wagons, the eye magnets.

Never, ever—under any circumstances—underestimate the power of . . .

. . . the Shelf.

37
My Cell Phone, My Precious

An active volcano.

A boiling vat of french fry grease.

The steaming bowels of hell.

That's just a partial list of things that are cooler—much cooler—than the state of Florida is in July. Midsummer temps there regularly reach 95 degrees, and it ain't a dry heat. Rather, it's a *sopping wet* heat. Like a sauna, if that sauna was full of mosquitos. And snakes. And alligators.

Also spiders. BIG spiders.

But as I've mentioned a time or ten, I love Florida in spite of all the ways it tries to kill me, and love sometimes clouds my judgment. This is a lesson I wish I'd learned in my 20s.

So recently, with my judgment duly clouded, I made the wise, wise decision to take my family to Florida in July. Not only that, I asked my best friend and her family to go.

"Won't it be hot?" asked the Hobo.

"And humid?" added the Husband.

"But guys," I said, ever the idiot/optimist, "we'll be in the ocean or the pool. We won't even feel it! And we'll still have fun. It's still Florida. Both of you like Florida."

"I like Florida in February," said the Husband. "Not Florida in July."

We had several such conversations. Still, in the end, I won, as I never let the wants and needs of others come between me and a dumb decision. And after a grueling, straight-through, 16-hour drive, my family and I arrived at the condo on Saturday morning at 1 a.m. with absolutely no idea of what we were about to experience.

We stepped out of the car, and directly into what felt like a bowl of soup. Thick soup. Like, clam-chowder-thick.

"Sure is hot," said the Hobo.

"And humid," added the Husband.

I waved off their concerns yet again. "It'll be fine. We'll be in the ocean or the pool. We won't even feel it!"

Sweating profusely, we carried our luggage into the condo, where the air felt just as horrifying as it did outside. We cranked the AC and, exhausted from our trip, went to bed on top of warm sheets, where we–you guessed it–sweated profusely.

The air conditioner eventually did its job, and I awoke around nine the next morning to a much cooler condo. *See?* I thought. *It'll be fine.* I poured a cup of coffee and stepped onto the back patio.

Where I nearly passed out.

The air, still thick with heat, humidity and all manner of large, flying bugs, hit me with what I can only describe as a comforter.

A wet comforter.

A very hot, very wet, comforter.

Did I mention the large, flying bugs?

Even my beloved morning coffee was nauseating in that kind of weather. I choked it down and decided I could add July to the list of the many ways Florida tries to kill human beings. Snakes, alligators, spiders, and in my case, quicksand–these are just a few deadly Florida dangers, not to mention "Florida Man," an internet term for stupid people who do stupid things while committing crimes.

Despite the countless ways to die, I wasn't going to let a little heat keep me from enjoying the trip. I finished the coffee and left for the airport to pick up my BFF Amber, her husband Jim, and their son, 13-year-old Jimmy. I found the three of them smiling and sweating profusely in the SRQ Airport loading zone.

"Sure is hot," said Amber, rushing forward to hug me.

"And humid," added Jim.

"It'll be fine," I said, yet again. "We'll be in the ocean or the pool. We won't even feel it!"

We drove back to my crew at the condo, unloaded the car and lost another gallon of sweat. Clearly, it was time to get in the water ASAP. So we repacked the car with chairs, a cooler and an umbrella, and the six of us piled in for the beach.

Here I should pause to point out that our Honda CR-V, Black Betty, is not meant for six people. Five people tops, if they're kids. Yet four of us– the Hobo, myself, and both of the Jims–crammed into the backseat alone.

I cannot emphasize enough the wretchedness of this situation.

Take two middle-aged, overweight Midwesterners–myself and Jim Sr.– add two adolescent boys and cram them into a backseat, and you have a recipe for a rank, fleshy sandwich like no other.

Especially in Florida.

In July.

But we were determined to make the best of it because–beach, baby!– and soon enough, we arrived and jumped into an ocean as warm as bathwater. We swam. We frolicked. And as I predicted, we did not sweat unless we got out of the water. This we tried to avoid.

Everyone had a blast–until it was time to go. Then, we packed, dragged and loaded the beach gear back into the car, which by now was as hot as the surface of the sun. I resumed my position, smashed into the backseat with the Hobo and both Jims. From somewhere under the pile of flesh, Jimmy croaked, "Let's go in the pool as soon as we get back."

It was a terrific plan. So terrific that it became the rhythm of the rest of our days: pack, sweat, beach, pack, sweat, pool, and finally, collapse at the condo in the air conditioning. My prediction had come true: if we stayed in the water, we'd be fine. And we were fine indeed.

Until Wednesday.

On Wednesday all hell broke loose. It was all my fault because I made one of my patented terrible decisions: I didn't use my Shelf.

Puzzled? Let me explain.

I stuff my phone in my bra. Actually, as we discussed last chapter, I stuff lots of things on my Shelf and in my bra when a purse or pocket isn't available. Debit cards, computer mice, snacks, the occasional small child–all have ridden shotgun on my Shelf, inside my slingshot.

Now, you might say it's gross and unsanitary to put items into a bra, and you'd be right. But don't knock it till you try it, because I'm here to tell you: Bra-stuffing works. There's no safer or more snug location on the planet than the bra of a middle-aged woman because, unless they're loaded and have had a boob job, average middle-aged women don't leave the house without a bra. If we did, we'd trip over our own tits. No bueno.

That's why my bra has become my purse, or rather, my Phone Purse, as I call it these days. I don't go anywhere without it. I even make sure all my swimsuits have snug built-in bras so that I can carry my phone, my snacks, my kids, etc. to the pool and beach.

Which leads me back to Wednesday.

As usual, I'd carried my phone safe and sound to the beach in my swimsuit bra that day. But given my history with phones and water and Florida in general, I'd zipped it into one of the beach chair's side pockets before going into the water.

This also turned out to be a terrible decision.

But I thought I'd made a great decision because the phone, an iPhone XR, was brand new. I hadn't even paid for it yet. I'd also refused insurance on it, and listened to a Sprint representative solemnly warn me the full replacement cost would be more than $1,000, and that I'd then have to lease an additional phone. It was, in essence, a $2,000 phone.

Still, I figured that in the zippered chair pocket it would be safe, snug and entirely free of water and my old Florida foe, quicksand. And it was.

For a while.

Per our routine, the six of us spent several hours in the ocean, the phone safe in its zippered pouch. When the heat became unbearable again in late afternoon, we began packing up to head back to the shadier, cooler condo pool.

In a spectacularly boneheaded move, I did not return my phone to its Phone Purse, a.k.a bra. Because I'd been bending over to help pack up, I didn't want it to fall into the sand, so I made a conscious decision to leave it stored in the zippered pocket of my beach chair. I then marveled at my own brilliance.

What a great idea, I thought. *It'll be totally safe there!*

Again, I bring you my old friend hindsight.

Loaded down with gear, we all trudged back across the beach to the parking lot and piled everything into the car. Figuring it would be easier to grab my phone before we got to the condo, I rifled through the stack of chairs.

"Wait. Where's the yellow chair? My phone's in there."

The males of the group took this as an opportunity to harass me.

"There she goes," said the Hobo.

"You're addicted to your phone," said the Husband.

"Can't be without it for 10 minutes, can you?" said Jim.

It was too hot to argue. Anyway, the chairs were stacked to the car's ceiling. I gave up and took my position in the sweat sandwich that was the backseat. Surely the chair was back there somewhere.

Except of course it wasn't. This I discovered upon arriving back at the condo and searching again.

"Where is the yellow chair?" I asked, then added what I couldn't quite emphasize enough. "MY PHONE IS IN THERE!"

Everyone gathered around to dig through the pile of chairs. Red chair, blue chair, green chair, but no damn yellow chair–and no phone at all. In the rush to cross the searing hot sand and load up the searing hot car, we'd left the yellow chair somewhere on the searing hot beach–with my phone inside.

My brand-new, unpaid-for, completely uninsured phone.

Amber, Jim and I rushed back to the beach. I sprinted through the parking lot searching for the chair near where the car was originally parked, while Amber and Jim combed the beach.

But the chair was nowhere.

We returned to the condo, where I realized there was one bit of good news: My old phone was still in my suitcase. Maybe I could track the new phone with Find My iPhone on the old phone. Here, I was overestimating my skill set, because I had no idea how to use–or even locate–the Find My iPhone setting on the old phone.

Luckily, we had a seventh-grader to help. Jimmy quickly pulled up the app, and my new phone's location pinged with a throbbing red dot, right back at the beach parking lot where we'd just looked.

"It's still there," I said. *"Get in the car NOW!"*

This time, the Husband drove. On the way to the beach, I used his phone to call my phone and see if the thief would pick up, and texted my phone with an offer of a $50 reward for its safe return. Then, I had an epiphany.

"I bet someone took the chair and put it inside their car to hide it," I said. "That's probably why we didn't see it in the parking lot the first time."

Once again, we arrived at the lot, so I grabbed the Husband's phone, told everyone to text me on it if they found anything, and jumped out to comb the beach with Jim while Amber and the Husband searched the parking lot.

Up and down the beach, Jim and I paced, scanning groups of people. Again, we saw lots of chairs: red chairs, blue chairs, green chairs, but still– no damn yellow chair.

Oh, the humanity. I'd lost my phone before, and it was a lot like losing my hand. Particularly, my right hand. It was worse than misplacing a purse, or even the driver's license I'd recently lost. And because the phone was brand new, unpaid and uninsured, it would cost more to replace than it had cost for the entire trip.

The entire, cursed Florida-in-July trip.

Alas, the yellow chair was still nowhere in sight, so Jim and I gave up and began hiking back to the parking lot.

That's exactly when the Husband's phone pinged in my hand with a return text–from my phone.

"I have your phone."

The chair thief. Great! My stomach flipped as I replied. "Where can I meet you?"

"Make it $100 reward."

OK, this guy was being an asshole. But I wanted the phone back no matter the cost, and really, anything under $2,000 would be a bargain.

"Alright. Where can I meet you?"

At this, I was met with radio silence. A bad sign, I figured, as this jerk would likely raise his ransom yet again.

I waited several minutes for a response but received none, so I started the process of texting threats and bad words. I was just about to hit send when the phone rang in my hand with a call. This time, it wasn't Thief

Asshole. It was Amber.

"I found your chair and your phone!" she said.

"It's with some guy, isn't it? I'm texting him. Be careful—he's being an asshole."

She laughed. "No, no. Your husband is texting from your phone. He's messing with you."

"Oh really . . . " I said, vowing revenge.

"We'll pick you up where we dropped you off."

Jim and I waited by the restrooms until Amber and the Husband pulled up. As we climbed into the back seat, my future ex-husband laughing at his own joke, Amber explained that she'd found the chair underneath a car, where beach-goers had apparently shoved it in hopes of taking it home when they left. "But they must not have checked the pockets," she said. "The phone was safe and sound."

She handed it to me, and I almost kissed her. It felt so good to see my baby again. My lovely. My precious.

My $2,000 debt.

For the third time that day, we left the beach. I stroked my phone lightly with one hand and used the other to smack the Husband's shoulder as he snickered all the way to the condo.

Glaring at him in the rearview mirror, I realized I'd been wrong about lots of things in the past week: going to Florida in July, not using my Shelf or my Phone Purse, keeping an expensive item in a chair, etc.

But I'd been right about one thing. The guy texting from my phone was indeed quite an asshole.

38
Domestic Warfare

I have to pee, but I can't get up.

It's not because I've fallen. It's not that I'm sick or suddenly disabled or can't move or I've been tied up by home intruders who won't let me use my own bathroom. It's none of that.

The reason I can't get up is that if I do, all is lost. Everything I've hoped for, worked for and prayed for during oh, the last 40 minutes or so will be gone. Important things. Vital things. Things I for which I wait all day, such as *The Simpsons, Family Guy*, and that most essential of ALL the things–the remote control. Because the minute I rise from the couch, the Husband will snatch it. He's shifty like that.

It's rare for me to even have it in my possession. The remote is my own personal dodo bird–a rare and mystical item whose existence I sometimes question, caged as it always is in the Husband's hands because he wants to watch *all* the channels *all* the time.

Tonight, I lucked out because he'd left the remote naked and unprotected on the couch while *he* was in the bathroom. So I grabbed it as soon as I walked in the door from work.

I'm shifty like that.

"Oh, well I see you've taken over the remote!" he says, hands on his hips as he returns to the living room.

I raise my brows but keep my eyes on *The Simpsons* where they belong. "Listen, pal. You've had it since 3:30 when you got home. It's 7:40, and it's my turn now."

He throws himself on the couch. "Why do you watch all these cartoons? I mean, how old are you? Eight?"

"I will have you know, sir, that this is *adult animation*. But yes, I like cartoons. They remind me of being a kid when I didn't have any responsibilities," I turn to smirk at him. "Or a husband."

He frowns, but settles in beside me and pulls up the ESPN app on his phone. I finish the end of *The Simpsons*, watch a full *Family Guy* and locate one of my favorite episodes of *King of the Hill*. I should be happy, holding the remote and watching my *adult animation*, but I'm paying the price with a steadily swelling abdomen. And if I leave the room, I will lose, well, control.

So I sit. Pressure building, eyeballs yellow.

I should've thought about this earlier, as I pretty much have to pee all the time thanks to tons of water and coffee and a bladder that's been cheerily pummeled by two fetuses. These commercials aren't helping either, intent as they are on showing things like mugs of beer, giant glasses of pop and waterfalls. Thunderous, pounding waterfalls.

To keep the remote away from the Husband, I could tuck it into my shirt and on top of my Shelf, then run into the bathroom. Unfortunately, that's a really bad idea; I know because I tried it before. It ended with one remote in the toilet, two wet hands and a chubby middle-aged woman who, three days later, needed antibiotics.

Ooh, but I'm reaching critical mass here. I can't take it anymore. I got to go.

Waterfalls, man.

I get up, do my thing and return a few minutes later to find the Husband has–shocker!–stolen the remote. He's bathed in the light of the frantic, blinking TV, continuously switching between *American Pickers*, college football, and whatever dick flicks are on tonight.

What's a dick flick, you ask? Well, get your mind out of the gutter, because it's not what you think. Dick flicks are chick flicks in reverse. They're movies for guys who like movies. *Taken*. *Jason Bourne*. *John Wick*. Any single one of the 700 *Mission Impossible* films. The Husband has seen all of these and lots more many, *many* times, probably this evening alone.

"I see you've taken over the remote!" I say, approaching the couch. "What are you watching?"

"I got a couple things going," he says. "*Pickers*, sports, *Taken 2*."

I flop beside him, groaning. "Didn't you just see *Taken* the other day?"

"Yeah," he says, "but this is *Taken 2*."

"Haven't you also seen *Taken 2*? Like, dozens of times?"

He shrugs. "Yeah, so, what's your point? You can always go watch another TV."

He's right about that. We have about a dozen working televisions scattered around if you count the two old box sets in the garage waiting to go to Goodwill. TVs are so cheap now, and I keep buying them for the bedrooms, the sunroom–just about every room in the house. And the front porch. And the backyard.

Do not judge me. I have a problem.

I don't just buy them because they're cheap. I buy them in the hopes that I will someday have a remote and television of my own so that I can watch what *I* want to watch. A gal can dream.

But my efforts are in vain, because even with 12 TVs, there's an issue, and it is this:

The Husband and I keep following each other around.

For example, he will go into the sunroom to watch football, so I head out to sit with him. He gets up to pee, and I steal the remote.

Or—and this one will sound familiar—I go into the living room, and he comes in to be with me. I get up to pee, so he steals the remote.

He hates my shows and I hate his shows. He thinks I have horrible taste and I *know for sure* he has horrible taste, and still, we muddle through. We put up with each other—it's called marriage, and I look forward to many more years of sitting beside him in misery while loathing all the terrible shows he chooses to watch, again and again and a-fucking-gain.

Forever and ever, amen.

For now, I'll pull out my iPad, look at the news and probably nod off beside him out of sheer boredom. And despair.

Unless he has to pee again, in which case all bets are off and it's *Family Guy* until bedtime, sucker.

Which would damn-well serve him right.

Ah, love.

39
I Like to Watch

Real estate is the new porn.

It is for me, anyway. Every single morning for the past three years, I've sat hunched over my iPad, drooling like a pervert at photos and videos and scrolling, searching, seeking ever more . . .

. . . real estate. Like I said–I'm not looking at naked people. I'm shopping. Online. For a house in Florida.

I look at houses in Florida like it's my job. Like it's my purpose. Like it's my compulsion. And, just like any fanatic, I devote way too much time to staring at this obsession, spending at least 2.5 hours each day on the Zillow and Realtor apps. Bear with the photojournalism major as she attempts some math here, but 2.5 hours each day over the course of three years is . . .

um . . .

hang on . . .

carry the one . . .

more than 2,700 hours. Or 162,000 minutes. Or 9,720,000 seconds.

I think.

The point is when you spend 2,700 hours, 162,000 minutes and 9,720,000 seconds doing something, you get pretty good at it. So I consider myself something of a whiz. I could have used the time trying to become a better person by, say, volunteering, improving my writing or learning basic math. But, no. I have chosen to squander vast quantities of time to become an online real estate expert. Or an addict. You make the call.

I can't help it. I'm desperate. With several dozen horrifying winters under my belt and retirement just around the corner, I've got an ever-increasing urge to get the hell out of Dodge. I've always said life is too short to live in Ohio, but somehow I've still managed to spend a total of 50 endless years here. This is mostly thanks to the Husband who has steadfastly refused to move, worried about silly little things like his "pension" and "healthcare," when maybe he should have worried about "separation" or "divorce." I've always loved him, but I've always loathed Ohio's winters, and it's a constant internal battle for me to stay.

He is lucky he's good-looking.

So stay I did. Of my 50 winters, I spent 27 with him through ice and rain and icy rain. I stayed through blizzards and snow and freaking thunder-snow, and yes—thunder-snow is a thing. I wish I didn't know that, but I do. Oh, how I do.

I also stayed because the Husband told me that if I stuck around long enough, we could move—or at least snowbird—when we retire, to a place near the gulf coast of Florida. Hence, my Florida real estate addiction.

Now, are we retired yet? No. Are we financially capable of moving at this point? No. Is the Husband ready for it at all? No. But please. These are minor details.

Anyway, why should I stop searching for homes when I'm so good at it? Thanks to all my scrolling, I've located hundreds of wonderful places for us in Venice, Fort Myers, and Sarasota, Florida. These I show the Husband each and every evening. In fact, come with me on my nightly journey from the living room, iPad in hand, to where we'll find the Husband working in his office, a.k.a. watching *American Pickers* in bed.

"Look at this one!" I say, propping the iPad on his belly. "Two bedrooms, two baths, big kitchen . . ."

He glances at the screen. "That's nice," he says, "but we're not retired yet."

Unmoved, I scroll to the next picture. "Just look at the size of that sunroom!"

"Why are you torturing yourself?" he asks. "Why are you torturing me? We can't buy anything yet because we're not retired yet."

"OK," I reason, "but see, on the map? It's right by the beach!"

He removes the iPad from his stomach and puts it on the bed. "Again, I say, we're not retired yet."

If you repeat this scene every evening for three years, you end up with– ugh, more math. Hang on . . .

um . . .

carry the one . . .

. . . about 1,095 times I've shown him the iPad, 1,095 homes I've selected, and 1,095 times he's said, "We're not retired yet."

The Husband is not the only thing standing in the way of my house quest, the community rules of the homes I choose are also a problem. I'd thought maybe the whole Florida/elderly stereotype was an exaggeration, but I'm here to tell you it's a real thing. Apparently, only geezers are permitted to live in the Sunshine State, as almost every house I find in our price range is located in an age 55-and-over community.

Not only that, most of these places do not allow dogs, and those that do don't allow dogs over 35 pounds. Suzie the Meth Lab weighs 50 pounds, and as you know, Missy the Mastiff weighs ONE HUNDRED FIFTY-FOUR POUNDS. So even though I find great houses for sale every single day, we aren't welcome in the communities on account of our youthful 50-year-old bodies and big fat dogs.

It's a quandary. But tell me—you've been here for a while now. Do you think I let any of these problems stop me? I do not.

Reality: still never an issue for me.

Despite the many obstacles, I keep looking at my real-estate porn, ever dedicated to my mission of getting us the hell out of here ASAP. I scroll, search and seek; I hunt, pursue and explore.

Finally, FINALLY, one day last week, I found it. *The place.* The perfect place.

In Englewood, Florida. Two bedrooms, two baths. Four miles to the beach. A community with a kayak launch, that is *not* age-restricted. Dogs are allowed, with *absolutely no weight limit.*

This all seemed too good to be true, so I pulled up the address on Google Maps and looked at the route between the house and Englewood Beach. It was indeed four miles/eight minutes to the water. And what was the only business on the map between the house and the beach?

TACO BELL.

I nearly dropped my iPad. See, I love Taco Bell. In fact, love might not be a strong enough word for the way I feel about it. Lust, maybe; passion—definitely. I obsess over Taco Bell the way I obsess over Florida real estate.

Taco Bell is also the new porn.

I leapt off the couch and ran to the Husband's office, nearly tripping over the big fat dogs.

"Look at this!" I said, slamming the iPad down on his stomach.

"Ouch!" he flinched. "What the hell?"

"This is THE PLACE. I'm telling you, this is the ONE."

"You say that every day."

"No, I mean it this time," I said. "This one is perfect. Plus, it isn't age-restricted, and they allow dogs with *no weight limits on them.* And it's only four miles to the beach."

He sighed. "How many times do I have to tell you? We can't buy anything yet because we aren't retired yet."

"Wait," I said, flipping over to Google Maps. "See the map? There's only one business listed between the house and the beach. Look at what it is!" I pointed to the dot.

He squinted at the dot. His jaw dropped open.

"Taco Bell," he said. "Whoa. It's a sign."

At that, my heart thumped with hope. I knew it was still a long shot, but I also knew how the Husband's stomach worked. He quite enjoys Taco Bell, too.

We spent the next several hours debating, discussing and mildly arguing over what was clearly meant to be our dream house. Back and forth, back and forth it went between "This is it!" and "We're not retired yet!" and "But they allow dogs!" and "We can't buy yet!" Even though he loves him some Taco Bell, he was still pretty adamant that we shouldn't buy a place before we had aged to full-on geezer status, as required by law in the State of Florida.

I almost gave up.

As a last-ditch effort, I pulled up Google Maps to again point out the Taco Bell conveniently located on the way to the beach. When I spread my fingers to zoom in on the map, the rest of the area businesses and restaurants appeared.

Here, right here, I should pause to be thankful. The Lord truly does work in wonderful ways sometimes. Because do you know what also popped up on the way to the beach once I zoomed in?

Donuts, man. Dunkin' freakin' Donuts.

My head almost exploded with joy. I had him, then and there, right where I wanted him. That man absolutely lives for donuts, especially Dunkin' Donuts. What can I tell you? He's a police officer.

Dunkin' Donuts are his porn.

I flipped the iPad back around, pointing to his holy grail.

"Look," I said, knowing it was all I needed to say. "Just look."

His eyes widened. Then, he lowered his head in defeat.

"OK," he said. "You wore me down. You can call the realtor."

I leapt across the room to hug him. "Thank you, honey!" I kissed him, then noticed his worried, stressed-out face. *Hmm* I thought, *Maybe I should cheer him up*. "Would you like to have sex?"

"No," he sighed. "I just want to go cry."

I left him to his tears to call the realtor, who advised me that the house probably wouldn't last if I didn't put in an immediate offer, as many investors also were online real-estate experts like myself. Unfortunately, the agent said, these investors often buy homes sight unseen online, never touring them in person, because they are rich as hell.

We, however, are not rich as hell.

But again. Do you think I let that stop me?

I grew certain that if I didn't put in an offer, I'd lose my chance at the home. Finding a place that allows big fat dogs and people under 55 was like finding a unicorn–exciting, unbelievable and dreamlike. Also, as I've mentioned, I have Weber's luck, and I knew without a doubt that if I didn't make an offer on the house, some rich bitch in New York City would snap it up immediately, laughing all the way to the coast in her bitchy way.

I wanted to be the bitch. *I* wanted to laugh all the way to the coast in a bitchy way.

Many emails, phone calls and trips to the bank ensued that all involved ugh–more math. But eventually it came to pass that I purchased a home online. Sight unseen.

My friends, of course, were appalled. My co-workers were flabbergasted. The Husband cried again.

Because, really–who does that? Buys a house over the internet without ever stepping foot through the door? Besides rich bitches from New York, I mean? Normally, those of us from the Midwest are far too cautious, practical and broke for such tomfoolery.

Tomfoolery is a word we still use in Ohio.

The place could be a mess. Could be full of mold or mice or bedbugs or, hell–gremlins for all I know. It could have pythons in the toilet, gators in the kitchen or crazy neighbors who shoot at us with a squirt gun full of pee. These are things that actually happen in Florida. Google it.

Yep, buying a house sight unseen online is possibly a really bad idea. But, like so many other potentially idiotic things in my life, I done gone and did it anyway.

It's been a few weeks now since I made this maybe horrible/possibly awesome decision, and the Husband has either resigned to his fate or gone into some kind of, like, conscious coma over the whole thing. I decided to bring it up again the other day, while he lay in his office perusing sports websites on his Chromebook.

"I'm so excited about the new place! Aren't you?"

"Sure . . . " he said, trailing off.

"When we get there, are you going to carry me over the threshold?"

He glanced over at me–and my extra 30 pounds.

"No," he said. "But I'll hold your hand."

Close enough.

And so soon, we will pack up the kids, our big fat dogs and several of our formerly white couches.

Then, we shall drive them all to our new place in Florida, purchased sight-unseen on the internet the way you'd buy a shitty $6 iPhone charger from Amazon. Add to freakin' cart, man.

Bada-bing, bada-boom.

It could be a disaster. A catastrophe. A nightmare.

Or it could be the best idea I've ever had.

I will let you know.

ACKNOWLEDGMENTS

I'd like to thank my friend, mentor and editor Jeri Kornegay for editing and giving gentle input on *Black Dog, White Couch* without ever hurting my way-too-sensitive psyche. I'd also like to thank the talented writers who generously gave their support as I wrote this book: Jerry Zezima, Tracy Beckerman, Celia Rivenbark, Peggy Zambory, Janet Frongillo, Wanda Argersinger–and many more.

To the people and places of New Springfield/New Middletown Ohio: Thanks for the memories and for putting up with me through my Decade of Dumb.

To the hilarious, long-suffering Husband and Hobo: You each have a fantastic sense of humor about yourself, and I'm so thankful you let me harass you in the pages of a published book.

Most of all, I want to thank my Princess. You were so wonderfully supportive during and immediately after the publication of my last book, and you made sure–didn't you?–that I'd write again with your signs.
I love you, Laura.

www.ingramcontent.com/pod-product-compliance
Lightning Source LLC
Chambersburg PA
CBHW070550050426
42450CB00011B/2796